THE *Satin* MAN

THE *Satin* MAN

Uncovering the mystery of the missing Beaumont children

Alan Whiticker
with Stuart Mullins

First published in 2013
this revised edition in 2021 by
New Holland Publishers
Sydney • Auckland

Level 1, 178 Fox Valley Road, Wahroonga, NSW 2076, Australia
5/39 Woodside Ave, Northcote, Auckland 0627, New Zealand

newhollandpublishers.com

A catalogue record of this book is available at the National Library of Australia.

ISBN: 9781742573083

Managing director: Fiona Schultz
Publisher: Fiona Schultz
Project editor: Kate Sherington
Designer: Andrew Davies
Production Director: Arlene Gippert

10 9 8 7 6 5 4 3 2 1

.

Contents

Authors' Note

For legal and privacy reasons, the names of the people being investigated in this book, among other recognisable details, have been changed. Although 'Hank Harrison' is dead, identifying him would be unfair to his family and draw unwanted attention to places of interest before the police have a chance to investigate. Members of the 'Harrison' family, family friends and work associates have not been identified by their real names.

The most important thing to note is that we, the authors, as well as private investigator Bill Hayes and former detective Mostyn Matters, are identified in this book, and stand by the events and quotes recorded herein.

Introduction

One particular incident brought home to me the obsessive legacy of the disappearance of Jane, Arnna and Grant Beaumont from Glenelg Beach in 1966. In February 2006, I had just arrived home in Western Sydney from the Adelaide Writers Festival, speaking about my book on the unsolved case. It must have been 100 degrees on the old Fahrenheit scale, so I'd hit the shower to freshen up. I'd no sooner grabbed a towel when there was an insistent knocking at the front door. My wife and kids had stepped out to the shops, so I was forced to rush to the door, dripping wet.

Standing before me was a tall man about 60 years of age. His utility vehicle was parked out the front of my house and he was pacing up and down my porch. 'Are you the guy who wrote a book on the Beaumonts?' the man asked. He appeared agitated and a little wild-eyed. Somewhat cautiously, I admitted I was, and asked if I could help him.

'I've come about the children,' he said.

I closed the door behind me and stepped out onto the porch. 'What about the Beaumont children?' I asked.

The man said he had read a review of the book in the local newspaper. 'I know where they are,' he said.

I asked the man to tell me his story, as he continued to walk up and down my porch. 'I grew up next to Grant Beaumont in Western Australia,' the man said.

Having spent the previous year writing a book about the case, I knew that the Beaumont family had spent all their lives in Adelaide, and the likelihood that the missing children had grown to adulthood under assumed names somewhere interstate was little more than an urban legend. But this stranger in front of me had gone to a lot of trouble to look me up in the phonebook, and track down where I lived, so I didn't want to upset him while he was on my doorstep.

I was as polite as possible. 'You've heard about DNA testing?' I said, trying not to sound like a smartarse. 'This would be cleared up in a matter of days. Did you go to the police with your information?'

The man said he had told the police, but that they didn't believe him. 'What does that tell you, then?' I asked. 'The police don't believe the children are alive, but if they were, they would be easy to identify through tax file numbers and census records, let alone DNA tests.'

The man appeared to calm down, but what he said next absolutely set my head spinning. 'When I read about your book in the newspaper,' he said, 'I knew you were talking to me and I had to find you.'

I was hoping my family would not arrive home before I had a chance to usher this man off my porch. My years as a schoolteacher had trained me to be calm and rational in the face of an irate parent – skills I had sometimes failed to utilise – and I didn't want to appear angry now. 'How could I have been talking directly to you?' I asked. 'It was a book review, nothing more. I wrote a book about the missing Beaumont children. Read it if you want some answers. If you have any new information, go back to the police. I am not an investigator, I'm just a writer. I need to go back inside and get dressed. Goodbye.'

The man appeared to be placated and left quietly. But this encounter, for me, was an immediate lesson that some people, for whatever reasons, were profoundly affected by this case, to the point where they integrated their own hurts and traumas into the story of the missing children.

I had opened a door into another world. What the hell had I got myself into?

* * *

In 2005, a publisher asked me to write a book about the disappearance of the three Beaumont children from Adelaide's Glenelg Beach on Australia Day, 1966. A chapter I had written for my bestselling book *12 Crimes That Shocked the Nation* had been serialised in *Madison* magazine, and this publisher wanted to know if I could extend the piece into a full-length book.

My immediate answer was no, although I was very interested in the social and cultural effect that the case had on Australia. I had grown up during that era of the late 1960s and 1970s, when the disappearance of the Beaumont children changed everything. It was the end of innocence. Parents kept a closer eye on their children and the unknown fate of three kids, taken from a crowded beach, became the cautionary tale that I, like thousands of others, heard during childhood summers at the beach: 'Don't go out of sight. Remember what happened to the Beaumont children!' No book had thus far been devoted solely to the case, despite the efforts of many writers to capture the definitive story.

What I knew then about the events of that long-ago summer's day didn't encourage me that there was a book in it. This was an unsolved crime without a crime scene, forensic evidence or even a suspect. There was so much myth and misunderstanding about the case that it had taken on a life of its own in the Australian consciousness, with many theories about what had happened to the children competing against each other in the public domain. I also knew from firsthand experience that South Australian Police (SAPOL) might be unlikely to cooperate with anyone writing a book about one of their unsolved crimes; my previous approaches to SAPOL had been met with a wall of silence, and this case, I was sure, would be no different.

Finally, I wondered what a book on this case would really achieve. Many of the witnesses, the police who worked on the original investigation, and the journalists who covered the events were dead, and any attempt to write a sensational account of the crime would only add to the hurt and heartbreak of the parents, Grant and Nancy Beaumont.

The more I thought about the project, however, the more I warmed to the idea. The one thing I didn't want to do, and I was ultimately criticised for this when the book was published, was to promote my own theory about what I thought had happened to the children. I didn't see that as my job – the world did not need another theory about the unknown fate of the Beaumonts. I said to the publisher that if I were to write the book, it would be a chance to look at the impact the crime had on Australia as a nation and to finally put to bed many of the myths and misunderstandings about the case.

The publishers wanted to publish a book in time to mark the 40th anniversary of the crime, the following January. They already had a cover in mind – a dreamy beach scene with the unfocused images of three children playing near the water – and I worried about appearing opportunistic (another criticism I had to deal with when the book was eventually released).

By April 2005, I'd decided to go ahead and do it. But I needed a sounding board, someone who would steer me in the right direction during the research and writing phase of the project.

I first met Stuart Mullins when we were teenagers, playing cricket for Richmond in Western Sydney. Stuart was the son of an RAAF officer who had been relocated to Sydney from Adelaide in the early 1970s. We attended teachers' college together and became firm friends over the years, despite the decades he subsequently spent overseas, travelling and working. In 2005, he was running a highly successful recruitment agency on the Gold Coast when I told him I had been asked to write a book on the Beaumonts.

Stuart reminded me that he grew up in Adelaide and had been living in Secombe Gardens, near Glenelg, when the children disappeared in 1966. He offered to come on board as a research assistant, driver and confidante during the writing process, and his support proved immeasurable. He even offered to write the introduction to the book, drawing on many of his childhood memories, which gave the case a poignant context.

I could tell that Stuart had been deeply affected by the plight of the Beaumont family; it reminded me of the impact the case must have had on the greater Adelaide community, let alone the rest of the nation. While I endeavoured to maintain a measured writer's distance from the subject, Stuart was much closer to the heart of the story, and became inexorably entwined in our subsequent seven-year investigation, which resulted in the writing of this new book.

My initial concerns about lack of support from SAPOL proved correct. We met with Peter Woite, Head of Major Crime at the time, and Detective Inspector Brian Swan, who was in charge of the unsolved case. They declined to let us look at original case files and warned us not to approach Mr and Mrs Beaumont to interview them. Perhaps they were worried that we were foot-in-the-door tabloid hounds, but it had always been our intention to write an historical and factual account of the case, based on the original police investigation – we weren't going to mine the grief of the Beaumonts for the sake of some sensational book. But SAPOL told us there was more than enough material on the public record to write a book about the case without their assistance.

At the *Adelaide Advertiser*, Stuart and I were provided with access to newspaper clippings, which at least allowed us to lay down a pathway through the myriad stories – ranging from the factual to complete beat-ups – that had stalled and misdirected the case over the decades. The family of former SAPOL detective Stan Swaine, who became obsessed with the case and spent the final years of his life looking for a new angle in order to solve it, have been supportive of our research, as well as frank. His former wife and daughters told us the case had alienated him from them, and ultimately destroyed his life.

In my book, I discussed a number of suspects and their potential involvement in the Beaumont case, but did not name a chief suspect – because there wasn't one. SAPOL had not been able to name a suspect in forty years of investigation, and there was not enough evidence to 'nominate' one of four persons of interest circulating in the media at the time – Bevan Spencer Von Einem, Derek Percy, Arthur Brown and James Ryan O'Neill (born Leigh Anthony Bridgart), a former Victorian man jailed in Tasmania for the murder of two boys in the 1970s. I wasn't convinced that any of these suspects had anything to do with the disappearance of the Beaumont children.

When I spoke about the *Searching for the Beaumont Children* at the Adelaide Writer's Festival in 2006, I was very conscious of the fact that many people in the audience had lived through the trauma and suspicion of the original investigation, and I didn't want to lecture them about how important the case had been in Australian culture. During the Q&A at the end of my 45-minute talk, I was asked a rambling question by a person who identified himself as 'John Howard'. He was upset about the characterisation in my book of the late Stan Swaine, despite the fact that it had been drawn from interviews with the Swaine family, who were sitting in the front row in support of me, having finally been given the chance to tell their story. It was clear to me that some people still felt strongly about the case, many years after the fact.

The following night I addressed an audience at Marion Library. A group of mainly elderly men and women listened politely to my overview of the case, but I was thrown by a question from the floor at the end of the night. A woman politely asked, 'What chance is there that the children are still here in Glenelg?' There hadn't been a thorough house-to-house search at the time, she said, and because many people still resided in family homes built a hundred years ago, it was possible that this might be the reason the children's remains were not found. I had made that exact point in the book – that the children could have been lured to a house no too far from where they disappeared – but was surprised a member of the public, and one who lived so close to Glenelg, had held the same view for so many years.

I also appeared on several radio stations around the country to promote the book. After one hour-long interview, the interviewer shook my hand and, off air, said matter-of-factly, 'I know who is responsible for taking the children. He was the father of a friend of mine and he's lived with this secret all his life.' I had heard this so many times over the previous six months that I hardly batted an eyelid. The reason I wrote the book in the first place was to dismiss rogue theories about the case, yet here was a journalist ignoring everything I'd just explained about the case, hanging on to his own theory. 'Perhaps you should write a book,' I said facetiously.

Invited to appear on the Bert Newton Morning Show on Channel 10, I was sitting in the green room before the interview when crime journalist Andrew Rule came up to introduce himself. I had read a lot of Andrew's articles over the years, and we'd shared the same publisher several years back, so we had something in common. I was concerned Andrew had been invited on to the show as a counterpoint, to pick apart what I had written on live TV, but he was very gracious and said I had written a solid account of the investigation, which stated plainly that Mr and Mrs Beaumont were not involved in their children's disappearance, that Dutch clairvoyant Gerard Croiset was a fake, and that it was impossible that Jane, Arnna and Grant Beaumont were alive.

One criticism of the book was that it was too parochial in writing about the 'Adelaide context' of the crimes – the fact that the city was the first non-convict colony to be established in Australia; that Adelaide, even today, has a particularly unique social class system; and that the city has produced many bizarre crimes, including the Beaumont children's disappearance, the Adelaide Oval abductions, the Truro Murders, the Family Murders and the Snowtown Murders. In my view, I was trying to explore the social and cultural forces at play, which not only made possible the disappearance of three children from a crowded beach, but worked against the case being solved.

Many people contacted me, as well as my friend and researcher, Stuart, after the publication of *Searching for the Beaumont Children*. On every occasion, we listened politely to their various stories – tales of abusive parents, paedophile rings and government conspiracies. Some of the people we spoke to were private investigators, others lawyers and former detectives, but most were amateur sleuths with a theory to push. I would always tell the person on the other end of the telephone the same thing I'd told the wild-eyed stranger on my front porch – take any information you have to the police.

'I am not an investigator,' I'd say calmly, 'I'm just a writer.'

Then, in June 2006, I received a phone call from a woman in

Queensland. She told me her name was Amanda and that she had been married to a man who was a teenager in Glenelg when the Beaumont children disappeared. As a child, her ex-husband had been abused by his father, and he'd always believed his father was involved with the disappearance.

'What makes you say that?' I asked, resisting the temptation to hang up on her.

'Because my ex-father-in-law's house was close to where the children were last seen playing, and within walking distance of Wenzel's Cakes,' she said.

My ears pricked.

'And one more thing,' she added, 'my ex-husband knows where his father buried the children.'

Chapter 1

26 January 1966

It was late January and Grant 'Jimmy' Beaumont didn't want to go back to work. The forty-year-old war veteran had given up his taxi run to try his hand as a salesman for the Lincot Linen Company, and in the week before the Australia Day long weekend in 1966, he was due to visit clients in the Adelaide Hills on an overnight trip. He had enjoyed his holiday over Christmas and New Year, spending his days playing with his three young children – Jane, Arnna and Grant – at the Somerton Park home he shared with his wife, Nancy. On hot summer days, he would take the kids down to Glenelg Beach, where they would play in the calm waters at the side of the then-disused jetty, and sit in the shade on Colley Reserve.

His kids could not get the beach out of their system. They talked their father into dropping them off at Glenelg Beach on his way to work on Tuesday 25 January. The children would catch the bus home from Moseley Street, as they had done countless times before with their parents. Jane, the eldest at age 9, was a competent swimmer, but the younger two – Arnna, 7, and Grant, 4, could not swim. This was Australia in the 1960s, though, a safe place for children, especially on a crowded beach. 'Don't go in deep water. Don't talk to any strangers,' Grant Beaumont told them, after agreeing to take them to the beach. Once he'd dropped them off, he watched them for at least half an hour, from a place where they couldn't see him. They were playing with other children and he left feeling confident they'd be okay.

The next day, Wednesday 26 January – Australia Day – was not a public holiday in 1966. At that time, the holiday was always celebrated on the following weekend. Just as they do now, many Australians took advantage of this traditional 'long weekend' by going on trips to the beach or the bush. The temperature was expected to reach the century mark that day (nearly 38 degrees Celsius), and Glenelg would be packed with locals taking advantage of the beach, as well as thousands of tourists visiting the city, which was hosting the fourth Ashes cricket Test.

As soon as the three Beaumont children woke that Wednesday morning, they wanted to go to the beach again. With school recommencing the following week, they were keen to make the most of the final days of their holidays. Filled with confidence after their adventure the previous day, the children asked their mother if they could ride their bikes to Broadway, at the top of Jetty Road, and then walk down to the beach. Mrs Beaumont didn't like that idea. Instead, she said the children could take the bus from Diagonal Road–Harding Road bus stop, as long as they were home at midday, before it got too hot. Nancy Beaumont suffered in the heat, and would not go with them that day.

After breakfast, the children got ready to catch the 10.00am bus to Glenelg. Jane wore pink one-piece bathers, pale green shorts and tartan canvas sandshoes with white soles. She was old enough to dress herself; her mother could not recall if she wore a ribbon or tortoiseshell hair band. Arnna wore one-piece red and white striped bathers, tan shorts and tan sandals, with a bright orange hair band. Grant, the youngest, wore only green and white bathers under green cotton shorts and red leather sandals. Mrs Beaumont later explained her son did not wear a singlet or shirt to the beach because it was hot, and the little ones 'wouldn't be bothered' with too many clothes. Anyway, she reasoned, they would be home in a couple of hours. Jane also carried a blue 'airways type' shoulder bag, with three towels inside.

Nancy gave her eldest daughter eight shillings and sixpence – about 85 cents, or $10.00 in today's money – for their bus fare and to buy some lunch. As Jane placed the money into a small, white clip-purse, Mrs Beaumont told them to buy a pastie from the bakery with the change, and bring it home for her. Lastly, Jane took a paperback, *Little Women*, to read on the bus.

Shortly before 10.00am, Nancy Beaumont stood at her front gate, at the corner of Harding and Petersen Streets, waving goodbye to her children as they walked the hundred yards to the bus stop on Diagonal Road. The bus driver later remembered the children getting on the bus, but could not recall where they hopped off. It is assumed the children got off the bus at the Jetty Road–Moseley Street stop, outside the shop called Wenzel's Cakes, and walked down to the beach from there, because a number of eyewitnesses saw them there between 10.15am and midday.

Mr Tom Patterson, the local postman, saw the children 'holding hands and laughing' in Jetty Road. 'It's the postie,' little Grant called out as they waved to him. At the time, Patterson could not recall whether he'd seen the children at the beginning of his rounds, at 10.15am, or at the end, at 2.55pm, but this was later established in investigations by police, who checked Mr Patterson's shift for the day, and determined the sighting had definitely been in the morning.

A school friend of Jane's saw the three children at Glenelg Beach shortly after 11.00am. They were swimming in the shallows near the

Glenelg jetty, then running up to Colley Reserve, directly behind the Holdfast Bay Sailing Club on Moseley Square. Colley Reserve was a quiet corner of the foreshore, between the sailing club and the row of sideshows, to the northeast of the beach. The children laid out their towels near two large trees and were running in and out of the sprinklers.

A 74-year-old Glenelg woman saw the children 'frolicking' with a tall, thin man at Colley Reserve. The elderly woman saw the man talk to the children and very soon they were playing with him. Arnna and Grant were jumping over him as he lay on the grass, while Jane was flicking him with her towel. They were still laughing and playing together when the woman left the area, shortly before noon.

The man was originally described as a 'sun-tanned surfie' or 'beachcomber', about 6 feet 1 in in height, and 30 to 40 years old, with 'blond' hair that was 'in need of cutting'. This description was later corrected by other witnesses. In a time when 25 percent of the population of Adelaide was composed of immigrants, it was noted that the man spoke with an Australian accent. The man had been lying face down on his towel on the grass area, watching the children as they washed the sand off under the sprinklers. He was wearing sky-blue bathers with a white stripe down each side and had placed his clothes on a white seat near the sailing club.

Around midday, an elderly couple, sitting nearby with their teenage granddaughter, had a conversation with the man. The man was with the three children, on the grassy area behind them, when he approached and asked, 'Did any of you people see anyone with our clothes? We've had some money taken …' The elderly couple were able to describe the children's clothing, including the shoulder bag Jane had been carrying, also confirmed by a middle-aged woman sitting nearby, who thought the man said, 'Have you seen anyone messing with our clothes? Our money has been pinched.' Later there was cause to wonder: Did someone really take their money, or did the man take Jane's purse so that he had a reason to offer them some money and a lift home?

The middle-aged woman watched the man as he helped the children put their shorts on over their bathers. She thought it was especially strange that he did this for the eldest girl, who appeared old enough to dress herself.

They had already missed the midday bus and now, according to the man seen with them, had no money to buy their lunches or get home. Having apparently won the confidence of the children, the man left them for a while and went to the changing sheds to get dressed. The children crossed the path that cut through Colley Reserve and stood near a seat, waiting for the man to return. They were still standing there when the elderly couple left the beach with their granddaughter at 12.15pm.

The last sighting of the three children was in Wenzel's Cakes on Moseley Street, where they were due to catch the bus home. A shop assistant later said the three children came in around midday and bought their lunches – pies and pasties, but also another lunch in a separate bag – with a £1 note. This information was not circulated in the press at the time and not officially confirmed by the police for another 12 months. The children had left home with only eight shillings and sixpence, so it appeared someone, most likely the man they were seen playing with, had given them a considerable amount of money to buy their lunch.

Although it was later erroneously reported that the children were last seen in the company of the man at about 1.45pm, the shop assistant in Wenzel's Cakes who served the children did not corroborate this account, as she did not see a man with them.

After the children left the shop, no one saw them get into a car or walk home to Somerton Park, and the bus driver did not see them on his bus that afternoon. As the police later observed, it was as if they'd 'disappeared into thin air'.

* * *

With her children away at the beach that Wednesday morning, Nancy Beaumont rode her bike to the other side of Diagonal Road, to visit a girlfriend. She left for home just before midday in order to meet her children, who were due home. When they were not on the midday bus, she wasn't particularly worried. There was another bus at 2.00pm and she was sure her kids would be on it.

Later that afternoon, some friends dropped over to Nancy's house unexpectedly. They enjoyed a drink together and talked throughout the afternoon, but when the children didn't walk through the door at 2.00pm, Nancy started to worry. Her friends offered to go with her to look for them, but the children could be walking home via any number of routes – along Moseley Street, Partridge Street or Brighton Road – and if the adults were out looking, no one would be in when the children arrived home. They decided to wait until 3.00pm, but there was still no sign of them.

Nancy began to think the worst – that the children had been in some sort of an accident at the beach. Surely they would have heard something by now, her friends reassured her. Glenelg was a 'safe' swimming beach, and if one child was hurt, her other children would have given the St John's Ambulance service their family details, and she would have been contacted. There was safety in numbers, Nancy told herself.

Grant Beaumont arrived home unexpectedly, shortly after 3.00pm; he usually came back from his overnight trips on Thursdays, but his clients in Snowtown had still been away on holidays. He knew his children would want to go to the beach, so he decided to come home a day early.

Nancy told him the children had not returned home from their morning at the beach. Maybe there had been an accident, she worried. Grant calmed his wife and immediately drove down to Glenelg, but the heat had drawn thousands of people to the beach. Mr Beaumont later remarked that there were so many people, he might not have seen his children, even if they had been there.

Grant rushed home again, hoping he had somehow missed his kids walking home, but there was still no sign of them. Nancy came with him when he went out searching for them a second time. They went up and down the coast, from Glenelg to Somerton. It was not until just before 6.00pm – almost six hours after the children were last seen – that Mr and Mrs Beaumont contacted police. Only then did the thought that someone could have taken their children enter their minds.

The Glenelg police station was situated in Moseley Square, not 100 metres from where the children had been playing at Colley Reserve. Two officers were on duty that day, one of whom was Detective Constable Mostyn Matters. The Beaumonts were 'visibly upset' when they spoke to Matters at the front desk at Glenelg CIB, he later recalled. Matters took a full description of what the children had been wearing, details of their ages and heights, and then rang the head office in Adelaide, while the worried parents waited at the station.

The heat that day was relentless. When the Beaumonts arrived home just before sunset, it was still almost 38 degrees. Grant immediately went out by himself to look for the children again, while Nancy waited at home, hoping against hope that the children would appear. There was eventually a knock on the door, but it was uniformed police, who asked her to tell them exactly what had happened. The police also searched the house thoroughly, standard procedure in a missing children's case, to rule out whether the children had returned home and were hiding from their parents, afraid they might be in trouble for being late. The children had never done anything like that before, Nancy said, but the police asked her to trust them. They were experienced at searching for missing children, they told her.

As night descended, the reality of what might have happened started to sink in. The children were never out at night, Mr and Mrs Beaumont said. The younger children were frightened of the dark. There could only be one reason the kids didn't come home, they realised – somebody was stopping them.

News of three children gone missing from Glenelg Beach interrupted radio and television programming at about 10.00pm that night. Friends and neighbours arrived at the Beaumont house and offered to help in the search. Some among the search party knew the Beaumonts personally. Others had heard the news on the radio and wanted to help in some way. Nancy was in a state of shock by then; she 'looked through people' when she spoke to them.

While his wife was comforted by neighbours and friends, Grant Beaumont went on looking for the children throughout the night. The streets were dark and Mr Beaumont couldn't imagine his young kids wandering around at night by themselves. The worried father rode in police patrol cars with amplifiers blaring: 'Have you seen three small children?' He walked along the beach at Seacliff, Brighton and Somerton, right along to Glenelg, but it was such a hot night that thousands of people were still on the beach at midnight.

Grant Beaumont did not sleep that night, and in fact would not for several nights to come. The police took him home just before sunrise, but he got into his own car and continued searching alone. As morning dawned with no trace of her children, Nancy Beaumont was in such an anxious state that a doctor had to be called. Dr Cowling, a local GP who had treated the Beaumont children for coughs and colds, sedated Mrs Beaumont for much of the next fortnight as the investigation swung into full gear. Mr Beaumont vowed he wouldn't go to bed until he found his children, until the family doctor prescribed sleep for the exhausted father.

The first night, the Police Emergency Operations Group was called into the search. Five boats from the Sea Rescue Squadron headed out from Patawalonga Boat Haven, sweeping searchlights across the water and onto Glenelg Beach. At 5.00am, the police launch *William Fisk* set out and searched the shoreline from Glenelg to Aldinga in the north, and back to Henley Beach. Police checked hollows and caves in seaside cliffs for any evidence of a cave-in, while others searched stormwater drains that opened into the sea. Members of the Police Aqualung Squad searched the Patawalonga Boat Haven, immediately south of where the children were last seen playing, but murky water hampered their efforts.

Police from city and suburban patrols joined the search the following morning, looking in backyards and checking sheds. Police cadets were called in to comb the sandhills behind the Glenelg Treatment Works, all the way up to the West Beach Caravan Park. A telephone was installed at the Beaumont's home so police could contact the family directly and keep them in touch with the investigation.

The day after the children went missing, an increasingly emotional Grant Beaumont spoke to Adelaide media in the front yard of his home, to make a public appeal for the return of his children. 'Somebody must be holding them against their will. They would otherwise have come home by now,' he said.

Some wondered if this could be true. Perhaps if there had only been one child missing – but who would think, in a million years, that someone would kidnap three children?

Chapter 2

The Phone Call

In June 2006, I received a phone call that ultimately changed everything we knew about the case. In that phone call, I talked to Amanda Harrison for almost an hour. She said she was a nurse, who had met her now ex-husband, Warwick, while they were both living in Queensland in the 1990s. They had both been married before, and had their own children already. After ten years together – a difficult period punctuated by her husband's growing alcohol and prescription drug dependency, and an escalating physical and mental breakdown after he revealed he'd been sexually abused by his father – she regretfully ended their marriage.

'My ex-husband is not in my life any more and I haven't had contact with him for 12 months,' Amanda told me. 'Every now and then I would get an email or a phone message from him saying "We need to talk" but it just didn't happen. He is a very damaged person …'

Amanda had been a trainee nurse in Victoria when the Beaumont children went missing in 1966. She still remembered the huge impact the case had on the country. 'It was unheard of, three children being abducted from a public place,' she said. 'It was a real game-changer, along with the Graeme Thorne kidnapping in Sydney [in 1960]. Nothing like that had ever happened before and I particularly remember feeling how dreadful it was that the police never found out who did it and that the parents never knew what happened to their children.

'Until I read your book,' Amanda continued, 'I didn't piece it all together. I'd been to Adelaide with Warwick to visit his parents in Glenelg. My own children had been to the pie shop where the Beaumonts had disappeared and walked to the family house, then down to the beach. I was amazed how close it all was.'

Amanda gave me the address of Warwick's family home and as we talked, I quickly pulled up Google Earth on my computer, and typed in the coordinates. As the address came into focus, I mentally drew a line from Colley Reserve, where the Beaumont children had been playing with the unidentified man, to the house in question. Perpendicular to that line, I followed laneways across to Moseley Street, where the children were last seen buying their pasties. I then completed the triangle by running my eye back to Colley Reserve. It was the 'Bermuda triangle' of the Beaumont case ... the key events in the mystery all happened there. But what was the connection with Amanda's ex-husband?

'We were watching a television program about missing children,' Amanda told me. 'It must have been back in the 1990s. We were sitting there, watching it quietly, when Warwick said he always believed his father had something to do with the Beaumonts' disappearance.'

This was around the same time that Warwick had confided in her about having been sexually abused as a child, both by his father and his paternal grandmother, but it was the first time he had ever mentioned the Beaumont children.

'Surely you don't think your father could have done something like that?' Amanda asked him. She remembered wondering how would someone be able to deal with that happening. Her ex-husband replied, 'They are in the pit.'

'I asked him, "What pit ... at the family home?" He said, "The sandpit," and changed the subject,' Amanda told me. 'I always thought he meant the pit in the family garage that was used to service the cars.' The family car was parked over a pit, so that the oil could be changed and brakes checked. At some point in the 1960s, Amanda said, it had been filled in with concrete.

Amanda explained that she deliberately had little contact with her ex-husband's family. 'The more I found out about them, the more I was glad they were at the other end of the country in Adelaide,' she said. 'The relationship between Warwick and his parents was very cold and distant. I think Warwick deliberately kept me away from his father's influence – not that I really got to know him during my marriage – but my impression was that Warwick's father was certainly capable of doing something like that.'

'Like what?' I asked.

'Abducting three children from a beach and then disposing of them,' she said plainly. 'Warwick's father was a deviant. He was extremely wealthy – and in Adelaide wealth is everything – and he indulged in a lot of fetishes. The main one, which everyone in the family knew about, was his "satin" fetish. Warwick's father could not control himself around satin, because he was sexually aroused when he wore satin pyjamas or any other satin clothing.'

She added one more chilling note: 'He wore satin pyjamas on the nights he abused his own son.' Warwick had told Amanda that his father kept satin Japanese-style pyjamas, and fashionable shirts and pants, locked in a special room in a house that adjoined the family home, which he also owned.

I asked how could she be sure that the abuse happened. 'I did not imagine Warwick's nightmares,' she said, 'his hyper-vigilance if he was touched when asleep, or his later revelation that he had been regularly sodomised for about eight years of his life by his father

… it happened.

'The other thing about your book that really stood out for me was the £1 note,' she continued. 'I did not know the children bought lunch with a £1 note. That rang alarm bells for me. At the time it was an enormous amount of money.'

In 1966, the average wage was £21, so a pound was about five percent of a weekly wage, or around $50 today. 'People would still raise their eyebrows if a little girl tried to buy something with that much money,' Amanda said. 'Who could have afforded to give little kiddies a pound note to buy their lunches? Because a working family wouldn't have.'

'From a young age,' she continued, 'Warwick's father would give him and his friends a £1 note to go out on a Saturday afternoon and play at the sideshows, so he had the house to himself while his wife was out playing tennis … That's when he would dress up in his satin clothes and entertain himself. Saturday was his day to be alone.'

So far, Amanda had not told me her ex-father-in-law's name. Now I asked: Who was he? His name was Phillip Henry Harrison, she said, but everyone knew him as 'Hank'. And there was one more thing … he was dead. Hank had passed away a couple of years before, aged 85. That's all we need in this story, I thought, another 'ghost' to chase who can't speak for himself.

I asked her to describe Hank to me. She only knew him as a grey-haired old man, a shadow of his former self, but she had seen photos of him as a younger man … six foot tall, with blond hair, a slim build, a high forehead and thin face. He would have been 48 when the children disappeared, slightly older than the man seen playing with the Beaumont children, but he seemed to fit the general description.

I told her my concern was that Warwick's story about the Beaumont children might be a manifestation of his illness, and that he might have been projecting the events surrounding their disappearance on to his father. 'I don't think so,' Amanda reasoned. 'We come into this world wanting unconditional love and when we don't get it we get scared ... especially if that parent becomes very abusive. Although they are abused, children feel a great need to love their parents. Warwick was very protective of his father, and his father's name, just as Hank was extremely protective of his own mother and her reputation. She was the lady of the house, but she had a dark side. I don't know why Hank idolised her, but then abused children often have a love-hate relationship with their mothers ...'

'So in your opinion, was Warwick definitely abused?' I asked.

Amanda explained that, though she began her career as a nurse in hospitals, she had ended up working in a correctional centre for sex offenders. As a result, she'd learned a lot about the impact of sexual abuse, and recognised its lingering effects in her ex-husband. 'My experiences with my ex-husband and my impression of his father, Hank, was that Warwick was certainly abused,' she said. 'In a marital relationship, you get to know certain intimate things about your partner, but it wasn't until I read about partners who had been sexually abused that some of the things that happened between us finally made sense to me.

'His father, Hank, was an only child, but his mother raised him as girl for the first five years of his life ... I got to know Warwick's aunt probably the closest during our marriage. She was the older sister of Warwick's mum, Anya, and knew all about it.

'God knows what Hank's mother did to him when he was a boy. But then, the whole family was bizarre,' Amanda went on. 'The family home in Glenelg was very cold – it was more like a museum than a home – and I refused to stay there when we visited Adelaide. If you used a cup you had to put it back in the same place or Hank would go off. He was so obsessive-compulsive ... the whole atmosphere there was menacing.'

Amanda told the following story to make her point. 'When Warwick's mother died, Hank got really upset that we weren't going to stay there, so he offered us the house next door, which he also owned, and we compromised.

'Being from Queensland, I loved white nectarines, which were impossible to find, and Hank had a tree in the backyard. It was a small tree, with seven or eight nectarines on it, and because there were no cooking facilities in the house next door, we were walking to the main house for breakfast and I noticed the nectarines. I asked Warwick if his father would mind if I ate one, and he said no, go ahead. I took one to eat and the next day all the nectarines on the tree were gone.

'I asked Warwick, "What happened to them? I didn't see them in a bowl inside the house." My husband told me Hank would have cut them all off, because he wouldn't have wanted me to enjoy them. It was just total control.'

Before she died, Warwick's mother told Amanda that she had stayed with Hank all those years because he gave her enough money to do what she wanted … to go to the races, play bridge with her friends or spend all day at the local tennis club.

'When you have money you do have a lot to protect,' she continued. 'The worship of money was the modus operandi of how they operated. [They thought] anyone who married into the family was automatically after their money.

'When he and his father fell out over the family business, and his first marriage broke up, Hank paid Warwick to stay away from Adelaide … just enough money to keep him quiet, but not enough to make him wealthy. He "kept him", financially and emotionally, at arm's length. That's how I met him in Queensland, where we were both living at the time.'

Warwick's relatives told Amanda that all he'd ever wanted from

Hank was approval. 'He worked really hard to gain that approval when they worked together at Hank's factory,' Amanda said. 'Warwick won a big international contract once and Hank actually said, "I am proud of you son." Warwick said that was worth more to him than anything in the world.'

A successful businessman, Hank was always good at selecting the right person for the right job, she said, exhausting them of their talents and then discarding them. 'Hank set people up for failure and then bragged about what he did. Warwick tells the story that he once promoted a young man with children and a mortgage, sacked him, and then laughed about it in the boardroom.'

'Hank obviously had enormous power over people,' I commented.

'Sexual abuse is another power play,' Amanda said. 'He held that over Warwick all his life.'

Even though she knew that most paedophiles groom their victims and abuse them over many years, as Hank had done with his son, she came to believe that her father-in-law could have been involved in the murder of the Beaumont children.

'What more power is there over a person than to kill them?' she said bluntly. 'At first I thought it was bullshit. While I didn't like Hank, if Warwick thought his father had something to do with it, why didn't he go to the police? But I learned over the years that victims only reveal their secret to someone they can trust and who they know loves them. Most males don't tell anyone – his first wife knew nothing about it – and when they do speak, they do so reluctantly.'

As far as Amanda knew, she was the first person Warwick told about his sexual abuse. 'We were together for ten years, off and on,' she said, the emotion clearly audible in her voice, 'and I really loved him. I always thought there was a really special person underneath all that pain. I always lived in the hope that this beautiful person would be free of all the pain, but sometimes it's the pain in our lives we get used to and the thought of having that taken off you is too scary. Even to this day, it makes me sad to think we couldn't make it work.'

All of this was interesting, but a lot of it was circumstantial. The proximity of the family home to where the children disappeared was intriguing, although Amanda's theory about the £1 note was no more than that – a theory. But if her ex-husband had been abused by his father as a child, the fact that an unknown paedophile was active near where the Beaumont children went missing would surely be of interest to SAPOL, I thought, even after all these years.

Amanda had nothing to gain from coming forward, and did not want seem to want anything more than to tell someone what she knew. 'Perhaps you can look into it and pass it on to police?' she said.

I told her I was just a writer. I also didn't especially want to investigate, because the case was a big black hole that sucked everyone into it.

'Just have a look at what I've told you,' she said. She added that she would be happy to meet in person.

When I told Stuart Mullins about yet another 'Beaumonts' phone call, he immediately offered to meet with Amanda, as they both lived in Queensland. He offered to do some reference checks to make sure she wasn't another obsessive person with an axe to grind.

Stuart was also heading to Adelaide on business, so decided he would check out the family home she'd mentioned, and see what he could find out about Hank Harrison.

'But the guy's dead,' I told him. 'He's a phantom. The police are never going to investigate a dead man.'

' At least we have a name,' said Stuart. 'We've never had even that much before.'

Chapter 3

A Nation Waits

The day after the Beaumont children were reported missing, calls poured into the operations room of the Glenelg CIB. With descriptions of the missing children circulating across the state, any reported 'sightings' at the beach, in the suburbs and even in the city had to be investigated. Although police described the public response as 'astounding', the investigation was already struggling under the weight of information flowing into Glenelg.

The search was coordinated from the Glenelg police station by Superintendent J. A. Vogelesang. Sergeant B. Fuller coordinated the Police Emergency Operations Group and the Sea Rescue Squadron, and Detective Sergeants Ron Blight and Pieter Vogel were the investigating detectives at Glenelg CIB; Blight, a nuggetty ball of energy, was named 'Wings' by his colleagues because he waved his hands wildly when he talked. Blight and Vogel worked under the direction of Detective Sergeant Alex Palmer, the chief of the Adelaide Homicide Squad. The Superintendent of the South Australian Police, Inspector Norm 'Knocker' Lenton, oversaw the investigation as a whole.

Detectives questioned people on Glenelg Beach and showed photos of the three children to youngsters at the amusement park at Colley Reserve. Meanwhile, forty of Mr Beaumont's former colleagues from the Suburban Taxi Service volunteered to use their vehicles to search for the children. The taxi company later started up a public fund to support Grant and his wife while he was unable to work. Jane Beaumont had recently joined the Third Somerton Brownie Pack, and girl guides took to the streets on their bicycles, looking for the three children.

On Thursday night, Channel 7 took the unprecedented step of broadcasting the 6.30pm news from a mobile broadcasting van outside the Glenelg police station. Anchored by newsman Brian Taylor, they stayed at the search headquarters over the weekend and broadcast special appeals from Grant Beaumont and the police commissioner, Brigadier John McKinna. Taylor, in particular, became close to Grant and Nancy Beaumont in the early days of the investigation, providing private and public moral support. After work, Taylor spent long hours searching the Glenelg area for traces of the missing children. Their unknown fate became an obsession for him, as it did for many people who would be touched by the case; he continued to look for Jane, Arnna and Grant Beaumont long after he walked away from his television career.

Grant and Nancy Beaumont had many offers of assistance and took pains to officially thank all the volunteers and police who were coordinating the search. Friends who were caring for the couple appealed for people to refrain from visiting the family home, no matter how well-meaning they were, given how fragile the Beaumont parents were feeling. Grant and Nancy Beaumont, however, continued to answer every caller at their door. In one example, a man came by to drop off some religious pamphlets for the family and then started canvassing neighbours about the Beaumonts. Nancy asked the man to stop, but neighbours had to call the police when he continued knocking on doors. When Adelaide police threatened to jail the man as a public nuisance, he wrote a letter to the Commissioner of Police, demanding that the parents 'be investigated more closely'.

Another stranger called in to tell the Beaumonts that the Marist Brothers of the Sacred Heart College, in nearby Brighton, had the children hidden in an underground room. 'When he had said his piece,' Nancy told journalists, 'he asked me, "By the way, what religion are you?"' When Nancy Beaumont said she was Catholic, the man said that he was 'terribly sorry' and 'shot off'.

In the initial stages of the investigation, detectives explored three possible scenarios. The first, that the children had drowned, was quickly dismissed on the day they disappeared. Glenelg was supervised by lifesavers, none of the children's belongings were found at the beach, and the sea search on the first night failed to find any trace of them. 'I ruled out drowning altogether,' Grant Beaumont later said. 'The beaches were packed and the sea was calm. One kiddie, perhaps, could be drowned, but three together – I just can't imagine that. There would have been some evidence.'

The thought that the children had run away from home was also discounted. There was nothing in their previous behaviour to suggest it, and their young ages – Grant was only four and still wearing a nappy to bed – also ruled this out. They had never been missing from home before, Mr Beaumont told detectives. He showed them a note Jane had written to her parents two nights before, when she babysat her siblings while he and his wife went out for a few hours.

Dear Mum and Dad,

I am just about to go to bed and the time is 9. I have put Grant's nappy on so there is no need to worry about his wetting the sheet. Grant wanted to sleep in his own bed so one of you will have to sleep with Arnna. Although you will not find the rooms in very good condition I hope you will find them as comfortable as we do. Good night to you both.

Jane XXX

PS I hope you had a nice time wherever you went.

PPS I hope you don't mind me taking your radio into my room Daddy.

Here was a tight-knit, normal suburban family and there was no reason for the children to run away from home. 'They're very affectionate,' Nancy Beaumont later said. 'They're lovely to one another. If the other two were very keen to go with somebody, Jane would go with them to look after them, and wouldn't leave them alone.' Grant Beaumont referred to his eldest daughter as 'the little mother'.

The possibility that the children had been taken from the beach was considered the most likely reason for their disappearance, from the very first day of the investigation. Press reports describing the children prompted a 74-year-old Glenelg woman to come forward and speak to police about what she witnessed at Colley Reserve that Wednesday morning. The elderly woman was able to give *Adelaide Advertiser* sketch artist Peter von Czarnecki enough of a description for him to draw the first likeness of the suspect. This sketch of a man with a thin face, swept-back hair and piercing clear eyes initially became the defining image of the case.

The only problem was that the sketch relied more on von Czarnecki's artistic invention than the old woman's recollection. From the description the woman had given police, von Czarnecki prepared outlined the face of the man. The artist later went to Glenelg and had a second session with the woman, who agreed that the outline and structure of the face he'd sketched 'resembled' the man she saw playing with the children, but she could not recall the shape and colour of the eyes, or the shape of his mouth and nose. As early as 31 January – just five days after the children went missing – the Adelaide artist admitted to reporters that his rough sketch might not be an accurate likeness of the man seen with the children.

A Broken Hill man who had come to Adelaide to watch the Australia versus England cricket Test with his family also came forward, saying he had seen the man with the three children that day. Based on his and other eyewitness accounts, the description of the suspect was modified to a middle-aged man in his late 30s or early 40s, with a slim build and 'fairish to light-brown' hair, parted on the left-hand side. The man was neither a 'surfie' nor a beach bum; nor was he a teenager or pensioner.

Following the release of an updated artist's sketch, pictured in this book, the public inundated the police with tip-offs and by the end of the month they had logged approximately 1,000 calls. A man with a 'striking resemblance' to the sketch prepared by the newspaper artist, who lived in Glenelg at the time, was questioned three times by police – once at Adelaide Airport, another time when he was walking along North Terrace and lastly when the man voluntarily went to Adelaide CIB to clear up the matter once and for all. He was not the man seen with the children, and was the only suspect in the case's five decade history.

Police also checked the files of known sex offenders in the area, but found no leads.

Detective Sergeant Alex Palmer said to journalists, 'At the moment we see a picture of the man striking up a conversation with the children. Arnna, the younger girl, would approach anyone and held no fear. She would have frolicked with the man with her young brother Grant and when Jane, the quiet, sensible one, had her confidence bolstered, she may have joined in.'

Palmer asked people who owned packing cases, cold rooms and industrial and shop refrigerators to check them. He may have been closer to the truth than he knew when he added, 'There are many vacant homes – both old, ramshackle buildings in the old area of Glenelg, and new houses in the nearby suburbs – and the children could have been lured into them and anything could have happened.'

Mr and Mrs Beaumont were adamant that they didn't know anyone who fit the description of the man seen playing with their children that day. Mrs Beaumont expressed amazement at the revelation that a stranger dressed her kids in open view of other people on the beach. Jane would never let anyone else dress her, she told police, even if it was just putting her shorts on over bathers.

The man's use of the words 'our' and 'we' when he spoke to the elderly couple were of particular concern to the police. It gave the impression that the man was with the children, that they were a unit.

On Friday 28 January, police divers moved their search to the Patawalonga River, after a woman came forward and told police she had seen three children sitting on the steps of a landing on the river's edge at about 7.00pm on the Wednesday night. Although the woman could not remember whether it was two girls and a little boy – and the children told the woman that they were tourists – the police could not take the chance. Divers searched the river up to a depth of 14 feet in places, but found nothing.

On Sunday 30 January, Grant Beaumont made a heartfelt address to the Australian public. 'Today is a world day of prayer throughout Australia for Australia Day. I hope whoever is holding my children will return them.' The strain of the past four days showed, as the big man began to break down. 'My wife is not too good,' he said, struggling to hold back tears. 'She is still under sedation.'

The following day, Mr Beaumont asked the *Sun News-Pictorial* to publish his favourite photograph of the three children, taken on a country trip the previous October, hoping that it would also be published in Victoria. Mr Beaumont thought the man who took his kids could have taken them to Victoria; given the intensity of the police investigation, he was sure no one would have been able to keep them hidden in South Australia. If the photo of his children was published interstate, he thought, maybe a miracle would happen. He had lots of friends in Victoria, too, he reasoned, mates he'd trained with in the 2-74th Battalion.

'Maybe someone will see it and recognise the kids,' Mr Beaumont told pressmen. 'You can see Jane's teeth are a little more prominent in the front and the fringe of hair on Grant's forehead. And that's Arnna to a T, with the big grin ... well, we were all happy then.'

His voice broke off and, after five sleepless nights of worry, he seemed to snap. 'What sort of mongrel would keep children away from their home for that long?' he cried suddenly. 'Grant is only four and he'd get frightened at night. He still wears a nappy at night. Who could keep a little boy like that away from his mother? Jane is a very sensible kid ... She'd look after the little ones as long as she could. But it's been six days now. They must be so frightened. I'm not a religious man but the only thing I can do now is pray. A lot of people are praying for us ... if I could give my life right now for my kids to be returned safe and sound I would ... and no questions asked.'

A week after the disappearance, 60 officers conducted a house-to-house canvass of over 400 homes in the Glenelg–Brighton area. They stopped short of going inside and searching each house, or going into backyards. Meanwhile, at a meeting of the Glenelg Council, it was suggested that the Patawalonga Boat Haven should be drained so a more thorough search for the children's bodies could be conducted. It was conceivable that the children could have drowned, despite the fact that none of their belongings had been found. More sinisterly, the bodies of the three children could have been weighed down and dumped there, although someone would surely have seen something in that case. The haven, which covered a surface area of 70 acres but had an average depth of only five to six feet, had not been emptied since its completion in 1959.

After conferring with Detective Sergeant Ron Blight, the council alerted local boat owners to remove their craft or to prop them up to avoid capsizing, as the gates of the lock would be opened at 8.30am on 3 February. As the boat haven emptied, police on the *William Fisk* watched the flow of water and debris as it poured into the sea for any evidence of the children. About 30 police, members of the Emergency Operations Group, and 35 police cadets then conducted a shoulder-to-shoulder search of the boat haven bed, churning knee-deep in the pools of water left behind, often sinking up to their thighs in the mud.

Hundreds of spectators watched the muddy search from the catwalks of the lock and the banks of the haven. Police used poles to probe the mud, while divers explored the deeper pools of water. In the afternoon the team of exhausted men continued the search upstream of the Patawalonga River, but found nothing relating to the children. The haven refilled at the next high tide.

On the day the boat haven was drained, Nancy Beaumont spoke to the press for the first time. Sitting at a small table in the shade of her fruit trees, in the backyard of their Somerton Park bungalow, Mrs Beaumont was comforted by her husband. 'I don't think they're alive, but I haven't lost hope, and all I want is that they come back,' she began. When her husband tried to console her, Mrs Beaumont shook her head. 'I've got to look at it at both sides, but it's the time that is getting to me … it has been too long. I can't be stupid and say that they're going to come in with a skipping rope. I've got to feel that the little things are huddled up somewhere and nobody has found them.'

She then burst into tears. 'I'm inclined to think it was all over on the Wednesday afternoon [that the children disappeared]. Whoever it was [who took them] had nothing to lose.'

Call it a mother's instinct or plain common sense, but now it appears that Mrs Beaumont was correct. Her three children were dead, likely murdered, before they were even reported missing, by the man seen playing with them on the beach.

* * *

Two days after the disappearance of the children, the South Australian State Government offered a £500 reward. Announcing the modest sum, South Australian Premier Frank Walsh said, 'We hope that as many people as possible will help wholeheartedly and join in the vital search during the long holiday weekend, and that this will result in the safe return of the children to their parents. The Government appreciates that the police are doing all they can, but a general search by the public may help to throw light on the question of whether the children are being held somewhere against their will.'

Following this announcement, Mr Walsh was contacted by a private citizen willing to offer another £250, but who wanted to remain anonymous. Dr Keith McEwin, an invalid pensioner, offered another £100; he could not help with any physical search, but hoped that his offer of a reward would prompt others to do the same. After decimal currency came into circulation on 14 February, the reward was converted to $1,700. Mr J. H. Ellers and Le Cornu's Furniture Centre each contributed a further $200, and a Melbourne newspaper took the reward over the $4,000 mark with a $2,000 donation.

In July, car dealer Barry Blackwell, a family friend of the Beaumonts, offered $2,000. He was unimpressed with the State Government's original reward. 'I don't think enough incentive has been offered to urge anyone knowing the details of the children's mysterious disappearance to come forward,' he said, from his office on Brighton Road.

The bulk of the final reward, however, came from Grant Beaumont himself. Mr Beaumont confirmed to a Melbourne newspaper that if information was brought to light that resulted in the return of his children, he would sell his Somerton Park home. 'It is a War Service house and I think my share would be about $4,000,' he said.

The total $10,000 for information leading to a conviction stood for decades. It was increased to $100,000 in the 1990s, then doubled a decade later.

Gradually, however, news of the missing children slipped off the front page of national tabloids and was buried inside newspapers. Australia had a new prime minister, with Harold Holt taking over from Sir Robert Menzies, who announced his retirement after 17 years in the top office, and the world moved on – everyone, of course, except the Beaumonts.

Chapter 4

Reconstructing Hank

In Queensland in 2006, Stuart Mullins sat at his laptop and typed into Google: 'Phillip Harrison, Adelaide'. He did not receive a single hit. He typed in 'Hank Harrison' – nothing, not even an obituary. Hank had only passed away a few years before, but there was nothing on the internet to suggest he had ever been alive. Hank's company had changed owners and its operating name; Stuart was able to find snippets about its history, but he needed more ... much more.

Working in the recruitment industry, Stuart had often used the services of a company in Adelaide that searched for legal documents and deeds of ownership. 'Anything from government records to real estate records, as long as it's legal, they find it,' he told me. He instructed them to look into any land titles Phillip Henry Harrison might have owned, as well as his birth certificate, marriage certificate and the contents of his will.

Stuart phoned Amanda, introduced himself and clarified some of the things she had told me. Amanda went through the story again. 'I hope you don't think I'm a nutter,' she said apologetically. In fact, in the end, she presented herself as one of the saner people who contacted us about the case – it was clear she cared about the health of her ex-husband, and had come forward in good faith to share what she knew about the unsolved Beaumont case.

Stuart needed to go back to Adelaide and see for himself where the Harrisons had lived. I wasn't able to make the trip, but Stuart said he was going there with an open mind and would let me know what he thought. When he arrived in Adelaide, he drove immediately to Glenelg and walked around the area Amanda had described. He could not believe how central it was to the area where the Beaumont children went missing, more than forty years earlier. Having grown up near Glenelg himself, little had changed as far as Stuart could see. Although it was a work-day, the laneways that led him to the house were very quiet.

The home was a large sandstone bungalow with high, concrete fences on opposite sides of the property, which didn't allow people walking in the lane on either side of the house to look into the backyard. The adjoining house Amanda had mentioned formed a boundary on the opposite side of the block. The house was not unusual in a neighbourhood filled with stylish sandstone, bluestone and concrete homes. Amanda told Stuart that the internal walls of the main house were made of cement, for insulation and to reduce noise. Even in summer, she said, the house was like an icebox.

Stuart spoke to a man hosing the front steps of the adjoining house. 'I used to live in the area and I think the Harrisons owned the house next door,' Stuart commented. The man introduced himself and said that Stuart was correct; the Harrisons, he said, once owned his house as well, and another at the back of the street, but that was years ago and there was a block of units there now. There had been a bowling alley at the bottom of the block, Stuart recalled, but that too was long gone. 'I remember this area from when I was a kid,' Stuart told the man. 'It brings back a lot of childhood memories.'

The man invited Stuart inside to have a look around his house. Stuart was able to look into the backyard of the main Harrison house;

he could see a number of trees, and a large gate that opened up to the back alley. There were two garages on the property – an enclosed area with a roll-down door, and another area under a large carport, with enough room to house a small boat. Stuart could not see any evidence of a 'sandpit', but the garage door was down at the time.

Stuart thanked the man, said goodbye and left. 'It was uncanny,' he later recalled of that day, when he stood in the street outside the house. 'The alleyway ran all the way from the beach.'

The next stop on Stuart's rounds was the factory Hank Harrison had owned, in an Adelaide suburb across town. 'I drove around to see where it was. It was where Amanda described, so that much panned out,' he told me. Stuart stood outside the cyclone fence and surveyed hectares of concrete driveway and bitumen, large production sheds and a couple of small offices, which looked like they had been built in the 1950s. Only a handful of workers crisscrossed the factory while Stuart stood there – this was no bee-hive of bustling activity, and it was clear the factory's best days were behind it.

Amanda had given Stuart the names of some of Warwick's bosses at Hank's company, and some family friends who had known her ex-husband when he was a teenager. One of the names on the list was Brian McHenry, the former financial controller of the family business.

Not surprisingly, Stuart found him loyal to Hank's memory. 'I went down to see Brian because I couldn't get much on Hank's business background on the internet,' Stuart explained. 'I called Brian and told him I was doing some research on Hank and his business, because the worst thing I could have done was to contact him by phone and say, "I'm calling regarding the Beaumont children." It doesn't encourage people to talk to you.'

Brian McHenry invited Stuart to his home and showed him three volumes of photos about the factory, along with some company reports, but there was scant material on Hank Harrison – a couple of photos of his former boss were all he had to show for the almost 50 years in which Hank ran the family business. 'Even Brian thought that was amazing,' said Stuart.

'I spoke to Brian about Hank's physical description in the 1960s and he showed me a formal company portrait from the period. It was just as Amanda had said ... Hank was about six feet tall, athletic but thin, with wavy light-brown hair parted on one side and brushed back from his face. His face was thin and long, with a large forehead.'

Stuart asked Brian what Hank was like as a boss. He was told that Hank liked to 'big-note himself' and be seen as 'a big man around town'. He also liked to carry wads of cash and was a big tipper. Brian described Hank as a very generous boss who looked after his staff, and they, in turn, were very loyal to him. His own children still remember the factory Christmas parties, in which Hank would shower the kids with gifts.

'He admitted he didn't have a lot to do with Hank socially,' Stuart noted. 'He didn't see too much of him outside of work.'

Stuart spoke to Brian several times on the phone after that, but always felt uneasy that he hadn't told him the real reason he was talking to him. 'I got to know Brian quite well,' Stuart reflected. 'I'd actually spoken to him on the phone quite a lot and when I met him again, I thought we had developed a good rapport, so I gave him a copy of the book, *Searching for the Beaumont Children*. I told him I was actually looking into Hank's background in relation to the unsolved case.'

'Thank God,' Brian responded, somewhat unexpectedly. 'I thought you were from the tax office.'

When Stuart explained that Hank's son had made some allegations about his father, Brian described Warwick as a 'spoilt brat' who would use his father to gain money and favour within the business. Brian said Hank bought Warwick a new car 'every year' when he was going to university, and later working for his father's company. Warwick was 'mixed up with alcohol and drugs,' even back then, he said. He was 'intelligent but unstable' and was ultimately sacked by his father. 'Warwick had a senior position at the factory,' Brian told Stuart, 'but rarely spoke to his father unless he wanted something.'

Brian was willing to provide Stuart with more names, and to introduce him to Norma, the family's former housekeeper who became Hank's second wife. Stuart again apologised to Brian for not telling him the real reason for his interest in the first place, but Brian said he understood. He too wanted to find out more about his former boss.

'Brian did say that Warwick hated his father with a passion,' Stuart later told me. 'He said Warwick was a bit of a "loose cannon" anyway, but admitted he'd always believed that the hatred was extreme, and couldn't be explained away as a workplace issue.'

Brian did a little digging around and located some photos of Hank at work functions, including one from the late 1950s, when he was about 40 years old – a formal portrait for the firm, with Hank wearing a stylish suit and bright smile. Another was of the factory management team, all in short-sleeved white shirts, slacks and ties. Another showed Premier Don Dunstan touring through the factory, and another depicted Hank, with grey hair and a tuxedo, at a factory Christmas party.

Brian put Stuart in contact with the HR director of the factory, who had worked with Hank for 30 years. Stuart rang the man, who said that he too knew Hank quite well professionally, but not much socially. 'He said it was true Hank didn't get on with Warwick and that he hated his father … that much stood out,' Stuart recounted. 'He put it down to either, Warwick was a spoilt rich kid, which it could have been, or that there was something more to it than that, but he was never sure what.'

Above: Grant, Arnna and Jane Beaumont in the backyard of their Somerton Park home in the early 1960s.

Left: Arnna, Grant and Jane, aged 7, 4 and 9, shortly before their disappearance in January 1966.

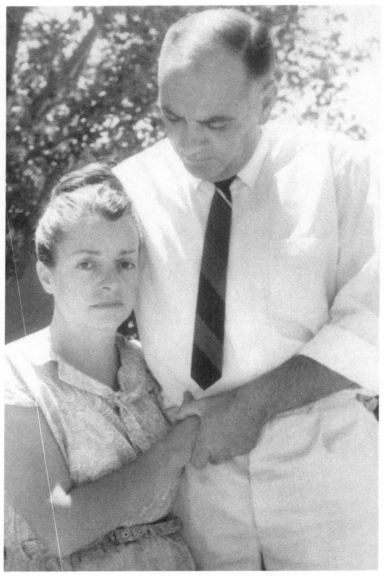

Nancy and Grant Beaumont face the media after the disappearance of
their children from Glenelg Beach. The grieving parents were hounded by
the press, religious fanatics and charlatans in the ensuing years

Sleepy Somerton Park, the suburb where the children lived on the corner of Harding and Petersen Streets.

Above: Glenelg Beach, where the Beaumont children disappeared ... flat, grey and serene.

Below: A rare police photo of where the Beaumont children were last seen playing, behind the Holdfast Bay Sailing Club at Colley Reserve. SAPOL

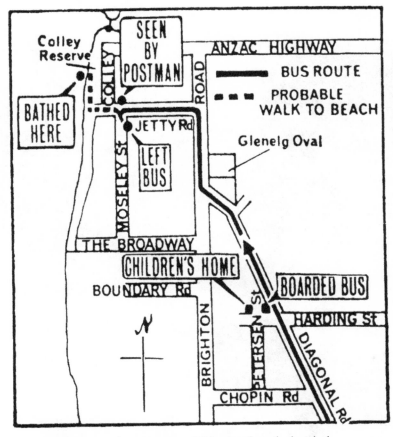

A map of the route the Beaumont children took to the beach that Australia Day, 1966.

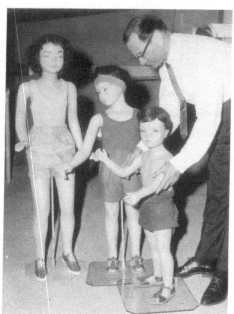

Above: Wenzel's Cakes, in Moseley Street, Glenelg, where the three children bought their lunch before disappearing 'without a trace'. Wenzel's, a Glenelg landmark, closed their doors in 2009.

Left: Mannequins, dressed in the clothing the children wore on the day they disappeared, were put on display to prompt the community to come forward with possible sightings of the children. There were none.

The initial artist's impression of the man seen playing with the children at Colley Reserve on 26 January, 1966. Note the man is in his 30s or 40s, with a long thin face and high forehead, and hair swept back off his face.

MISSING
BEAUMONT CHILDREN
SOUTH AUSTRALIA

At 10.00 a.m. on Wednesday, 26th January, 1966 the undermentioned children left their home at 109 Harding Street, SOMERTON PARK to go to the beach at GLENELG (a distance of about two miles). They have not been heard of since despite extensive Police enquiries.

1. **Jane Nartare BEAUMONT, 9 years – 4 ft. 6 in. tall. Hair: fair, ear length, s u n bleached, pushed back with a fringe in front. Two front teeth prominent. Well spoken but stutters when excited.**

2. **Arnna Kathleen BEAUMONT, 7 years – 4 ft. tall, dark brown hair with a fringe, suntanned complexion. Dark brown eyes, plump build.**

3. **Grant Ellis BEAUMONT, 4 years – 3 ft. tall, brown hair with a fringe, brown eyes, olive complexion.**

SUSPICION IS ATTACHED TO AN UNKNOWN MAN,

DESCRIPTION

Male, late 30's or early 40's, 6 ft. to 6 ft. 1 in., light brown hair long at the back with a part on the side, slim build and thinfaced, fair complexion.

Any person who can give any information relating to this matter is asked to contact their nearest Police Station

URGENTLY

Issued by the South Australian Police Dept.

The poster distributed by police in the wake of the children's disappearance. Despite the offer of a reward, no person responsible was ever identified. SAPOL

'People can have a run-in with their father,' the former human resources director told Stuart, 'but this was pure hate.'

The man knew Anya, Hank's first wife and Warwick's mother, and believed they lived separate lives. 'When they attended functions, it was very frosty,' he said.

The HR director had played golf with Hank, and said he was an avid swimmer at Glenelg Beach, who'd always looked fit and tanned. He also confirmed that Hank carried wads of cash with him. 'Hank was highly intelligent, a savvy businessman, but he could be very manipulative,' he told Stuart. 'You wouldn't want to cross him. His work and his company was his life.'

Stuart tried to talk to two other former managers from the factory, but they were clear that they wouldn't discuss Hank. 'That was strange, because they didn't even know what I wanted to talk about,' Stuart recalled. 'It was just, "I don't want to talk to you." Perhaps word of mouth had got around by then. I still had it in my mind to check out just who Hank was. He seemed to hang around in very senior but closed circles, private clubs. I learned Hank was also a Mason, for example, which I found very interesting.'

The HR director, who did not want to be identified, told Stuart that Hank was a member at a country club in Adelaide. Stuart decided to drive there and speak to the manager, who remembered Hank from many years before; Hank's company used to sponsor a corporate day there in the 1970s, not that there was any evidence of it now.

'The manager gave me volumes of photos to look at, dating back to the early 1950s,' Stuart said of his visit. 'There was not one photo in there of Hank. I found that rather strange considering he used to go there fairly regularly and his company was associated with the club. We went through them, page by page, and even the manager admitted, "I'm really surprised by that."'

Here was a leading Adelaide businessman, a millionaire, who was very well-connected in certain circles, but there were next-to-no published photographs of, or public information about, Hank Harrison. As one lawyer later remarked to Stuart and I, here was a guy who didn't want to be photographed. But at least it could be confirmed that he did, at one point, exist.

The legal searches Stuart had requested before his trip to Adelaide began to reveal more details. Phillip Henry 'Hank' Harrison was born in the family home in Glenelg. Hank lived his whole life in the house his father built, right up to the day he died in the early 2000s. He was the only son of William Harrison, who immigrated to Australia at the turn of the last century and served in the army. 'Bill' Harrison built and designed a large family home, which included a cellar, four metres by four metres, a necessary addition for any house in a time before refrigeration. Bill was regularly absent on business for the first five years of Hank's life, working in a government job.

When Stuart was provided with copies of Hank's birth certificate and the marriage record of his parents, it was clear he'd been born out of wedlock, a huge social shame at the time. Hank's mother Catherine ('Kitty') was almost 40 years old when she gave birth to Hank, and didn't marry Bill Harrison until two years later, when he returned to Adelaide from his travels. Their marriage was unconventional, to say the least. Kitty was a very domineering mother, according to Amanda and other family members, and Bill was an eccentric, often absent father, which made for a very unsettling upbringing for Hank.

According to Harrison family members, Hank's mother was so disappointed in having had a boy that, for the first five or six years of Hank's life, she dressed and raised him as a girl. She dressed him in satin, which was the start of a life-long fascination with satin products, especially pyjamas, shirts and dresses.

Hank's father died after accidentally swallowing poison in the

1940s. When Hank moved his own bride, Anya, into the house, his mother Kitty was still living there. She wreaked her own form of emotional and sexual havoc on Hank and Anya's son, Warwick, who was born in the late 1940s. Hank's wife was a Catholic, while Hank was a staunch Anglican, which added to the strain in their marriage. They were married for 50 years, until Anya's death in the 1990s, but always slept in separate rooms.

Hank was educated at a top grammar school, but left at age 16 to take on an apprenticeship with a local manufacturing plant during the day, and study at Adelaide University at night. He became a very wealthy businessman when he recommended that the manufacturing plant in Adelaide divide into two companies, and took over the running of the plant on the other side of the city. The factory grew to more than 100 workers in the boom years of the 1950s, and had spread out over more than 2.5 hectares by the time it was sold in the 1990s. Hank had also bought adjoining land, which had a number of houses and work huts on it, and leased the land to the company until it was able to buy the property from him. Renting the land to the company made him a small fortune.

After Anya died in 1994, Hank married his housekeeper, Norma. In 1999, several years before he died, Hank transferred ownership of the family home to Norma. The house itself was worth almost $1 million. When he died in the early 2000s, Norma inherited the majority of his estate, which was valued at more than $3 million. Through title searches, Stuart found out that Hank owned other properties, including some adjoining the company factory in suburban Adelaide, but these were all liquidated after Hank retired in the 1990s and his company was sold.

In Hank's will, Norma received a legacy of $1.5 million. Trustees of the estate and peripheral family members received differing amounts, between $10,000 and $250,000. Hank's son Warwick received no cash from the will, but was granted ownership of the house adjoining the family home, as well as all the furniture, fittings and fixtures. The house was immediately sold and the money given to the public trustee looking after Warwick's finances; at the time, Warwick was living on an invalid pension and battling prescription drug and alcohol issues. The will also stated that Warwick's son Joel would receive a sum of money on 'attaining 21 years of age'.

Was this the issue fuelling Warwick's hatred of his father? We could not afford to dismiss the theory that Warwick made allegations about his father because he was bitter about the terms of the will, and wanted money from his father's estate. But Warwick didn't contact us about his father – Amanda did. Did she have anything to gain by coming forward? Stuart was keen to meet her in person and see for himself.

Chapter 5

Red Herrings

In September 1966, the unknown fate of the Beaumont children was once again in the national news. A policeman in Kaniva, 257 miles west of Melbourne near the South Australian border, overheard a disturbing conversation when he dialled a 'crossed' line, while trying to ring his superiors in Russell Street, Melbourne. Senior Constable Bob Grose overheard a voice on the line say, 'We're bringing the Beaumont kids back from Hobart.'

Victorian police immediately viewed the incident as a hoax; it was impossible to get a 'crossed line' from Hobart when ringing from Kaniva, they said. Detective Sergeant Stan Swaine, newly appointed chief of the Adelaide Homicide Squad, disagreed with his Melbourne colleagues. 'We don't know for sure, but our investigations would point very strongly toward it being a bona fide call,' Swaine told the Adelaide media. 'We are pinning great hopes on this lead.' He said he would launch an 'intensive investigation' into the phone call.

Stanley Swaine was an 'old-school' police detective. At 6 feet 2 inches and 17 stone, he was nicknamed 'Tonner' because of his immense size and reputation. As a young constable, he had survived an early brush with death when he was stabbed with a screwdriver, before he shot his assailant dead. The physical injuries were easy to see – a scar over the eye and a nervous tic that made his eye beat 'like a butterfly wing' – but the psychological damage, which manifested in bizarre mood swings, violent outbursts and obsessive behaviours, ruined his relationship with his family and ultimately his career, according to his former wife and daughters.

Swaine quickly graduated from motor transport to the 'larrikin squad', whose job it was to break up groups of young people around Adelaide nightspots, then moved again to Homicide. At age 41, he was made head of the Adelaide CIB Homicide Squad, but was known by family and colleagues for his 'impulsiveness' and an 'unwillingness to listen'.

In September 1966, Swaine failed to heed the advice of Melbourne detectives and believed the 'Kaniva connection' phone call was genuine. Grant and Nancy Beaumont greeted the new information with renewed hope. Nancy spoke to Channel 7's Brian Taylor and appealed directly to her children's abductor. 'Please, whoever you are, please listen with your heart,' she said. 'I feel that in different ways you have been kind to our children, but I beg you, show a greater kindness by letting them come home. Perhaps you could let them go to a household or shop and tell the people their names and address so they can be safely returned to us. We do love and miss them so.'

On 10 October, Brian Taylor drove Mr Beaumont to Kaniva to meet Senior Constable Grose. 'Senior Constable Grose is a very sincere man and although he thought my children were dead before the telephone conversation, he is now convinced they are alive,' Grant Beaumont told the press. 'I am sure that whoever has them must have looked after them well, since it is now eight months and 14 days since we last saw the children.'

Days later, however, two South Australian women told police they were responsible for the conversation about the Beaumont children, but that Senior Constable Grose had got it all wrong. The two women had first discussed the case of the missing Beaumont children, but then moved on to another subject involving two other children, who had been on a holiday to Hobart and recently returned to the mainland. When Grose heard the conversation, the women were merely finishing talking about the Beaumont children, then seamlessly started talking about the Hobart trip.

The 'Kaniva Connection' was the first of a number of red herrings that would raise and dash the hopes of the parents and the greater community, time and time again.

* * *

During that first year, Grant and Nancy saw their children's birthdays come and go, with no news of their fates. 'These have been terrible days for us. Empty,' Mrs Beaumont admitted to journalists in 1968. 'Christmas was the worst time. All those toys. Other kids riding about on new bikes – you can imagine how empty our house was.'

The Beaumonts decided to get out of Adelaide for Christmas. 'We couldn't stand the house with the empty rooms,' Grant said. 'We started driving to Sydney but only got as far as Mildura. Christmas Day was terribly hot and we just couldn't stay in the caravan looking at each other … we got in the car and we were home by Boxing Day. But there was nothing at home.'

On the first anniversary of her children's disappearance, Nancy dreamt for the first time since she could remember. 'Last night I dreamt I heard a knock on the back door,' she told journalists. 'It was the children. They said, "Hello Mum." The only thing I said was "Where have you been?" They were standing there in the back lobby (of the house). I cried, and felt them all over.'

As long as their children's bodies weren't found, there was a possibility that they were still alive. 'Jim and I are both convinced the children are alive,' Nancy said. 'I know I said I believed they had been murdered the week they disappeared, but I was sick then. The doctor had kept me asleep. But if the children had been murdered, their bodies would have been found. You couldn't hide three bodies, and who would murder three children?'

'Our children are alive,' Mr Beaumont added. 'Nance and I would go mad if we couldn't believe that.

'So many things remind us of what happened,' he went on. 'It's with us all the time. Even when I go out on business. I talk to customers, and they know what has happened. There's not much they can say, but they feel they have to say something. I appreciate their thoughts and their prayers. But people can be vicious. There have been all kinds of rumours – for instance, that I am a member of [conservative Christian movement] the Plymouth Brethren or that I was the taxi driver said to have picked the children up from the beach – and some even more unpleasant.'

Some in the media and public had blamed Nancy Beaumont. Why had she let her children go to the beach unattended? 'All I can say is that the beach was the same distance away as school,' Mrs Beaumont said in 1967, 'and they went to school every day by themselves. The only thing I can think is that they accepted a lift from the beach because they had missed the 12 o'clock bus. I told them not to get into a car with anybody they didn't know, but if they missed their bus, they might have accepted an offer of a lift home.'

In November 1966, the arrival of the Dutch clairvoyant Gerard Croiset turned the case into a sideshow, with local media trivialising what had effectively become a murder investigation by even reporting Croiset's 'visions'. Then the following year, the unsolved case took another turn for the worse. On 29 February 1968, the *Melbourne Herald* sensationally reported that: 'Adelaide Homicide detectives made a secret visit to Melbourne this week. It is believed that Mr and Mrs Beaumont came with the detectives. They booked into a south-east suburban motel. None of the other guests recognised them. Melbourne police were not aware of the visit. It is believed the detectives were following what they believed was a worthwhile lead ... the detectives checked the lead and returned to Adelaide yesterday.'

What prompted Adelaide detectives to make a clandestine trip to Victoria with Grant and Nancy Beaumont? The true story, an incident that became known as the 'Dandenong letters', only came to light several years after the fact.

Earlier that summer, the *Melbourne Herald* ran a series of articles entitled 'The Beaumont Disclosures' as part of a News Ltd serialisation, to mark the second anniversary of the children's disappearance. In these articles, which ran over three days, Grant and Nancy reiterated their belief that their 'kiddies' were still alive.

They soon received the following letter, written in a childlike script in blue ink:

Dear Mum and Dad,

We are safe, so there is no need to worry about us! Oh, we really missed you in the last two years. At the beach on that day, we were walking to the bustop [sic] when a man in a car stopped us and asked us if we wanted a ride. I said that we did and that is how it all started. The man would not let us write before. He is letting us write tonight because he saw the story in the Herald tonight and felt sorry for you both. He watched us a lot for about six weeks and then he did not watch us so much. Arna (sic) and I often talk about you but Grant does not remember you at all after more than two years. We have been well fed all the time. I as well as Arna and Grant hope that you are both well. The man said to me just now that he will willingly let us go if you will come over to Victoria to get us as long as you do not call the police. He said that if you do the deal is off. You have to pick us up in front of the Dandenong post office at ten minutes to nine o'clock next Monday, the twenty sixth of February. You, Dad, have to wear a dark coat and white pants so that the man will know you. The man told me to tell you that the police must not know at all. He said that if you do tell them, you may as well not come, so please do not tell them. The Dandenong post office is in Victoria in case you did not know. We are all looking forward to seeing you next Monday. Please do not tell the police. The man did not mean to harm us. We still love you both.

Love Jane, Arna and Grant. (This is Jane who is writing.)

Swaine quickly became involved in the affair; he later said that he forensically checked the handwriting of the letter against one of Jane Beaumont's exercise books, stored at Glenelg CIB, and that 'many characteristics' were similar. Despite the fact that one of their daughter's names was misspelled, 'Arna', and that the writing did not match the handwriting style of their eldest daughter, for the second time since their children went missing, Grant and Nancy Beaumont were again filled with hope.

Swaine did not tell Superintendent Norm Lenton of his plans, but talked the Beaumonts into allowing him to organise a secret trip to Dandenong to keep the appointment on Monday 26 February. Swaine asked an associate to drive him and Mr and Mrs Beaumont to Melbourne in a borrowed car. They left Adelaide at 3.00am and once they reached Melbourne, changed cars.

Grant and Nancy booked into the Commodore Motel, four miles outside Dandenong, under Mrs Beaumont's maiden name, 'Ellis'. But Swaine made the error of booking himself and Bill Cotton under their real names at the Dandenong Hotel. Without them even knowing it, the situation quickly swung out of control.

A Dandenong police sergeant contacted Douglas 'Stainless' Steel, a former Adelaide reporter and, at the time, the chief of staff for the *Melbourne Herald*. 'Funny thing,' the sergeant told Steel. 'I got a call not long ago from a local publican. He knew that we have had a lot of safe busts around here recently and rang me to say a stranger had booked in at his pub and would I check him out. So I checked him out and found he was a detective sergeant named Swaine from Adelaide. I didn't know he was here, but he checks out OK.'

Steel knew Swaine was working on the Beaumont case, so he sent two *Herald* reporters to Dandenong to see what was going on. John Kroeger, the chief of staff for the *Adelaide News*, was also 'tipped off' that Grant and Nancy had left for Dandenong with Swaine to meet an unknown man, who was going to return the Beaumont children. He contacted his police roundsman Ken Anderson, staff writer Doug Easom and photographers Bert Stansbury and Mick Conrey, and the five newsmen rushed towards Melbourne in two cars. They arrived in Dandenong, 20 miles on the western side of Melbourne, at 5.00am the following morning, having driven through the night. After freshening up in a motel room, Kroeger took his men to the Dandenong Post Office and staked them at several vantage points to record what was about to unfold.

Some time before 9.00am, a van pulled up near the post office, which was situated on a sharp corner in the middle of the town. All five newsmen immediately recognised the man who got out of a light-coloured van, wearing work clothes, as 'Tonner' Swaine. At about 9 o'clock, Grant Beaumont took up a position in front of the post office – as instructed, he was wearing a blue bowling blazer and white slacks.

Alice Parker was working at the post office that day and remembered the 'commotion' when she was interviewed many years later. Mrs Parker recalled that two calls were made that morning. In the first call, a male voice asked in an Australian accent, 'Look, I wonder if you could do me a favour? Can you see a man standing outside your office, wearing white cricket slacks and a blue blazer? Well, would you mind popping out and telling him I won't be long?

I've had a bit of trouble but I'll be there as quick as I can.'

Mrs Parker did just that and the man was very thankful. When she reached her counter, she suddenly realised the man was Grant Beaumont.'Just after that, one of our messenger boys came from the telegram room,' she later recalled. The boy said he'd had a telephone call to tell a man outside that someone would be there shortly. A final, third message said that the young Grant was sick, so the party would be delayed until after lunch.

During the next six hours, Stan Swaine changed positions many times as he readied to 'scoop [the children] up and whisk them back along the Melbourne road to the motel where Nancy was waiting'. At one stage, Grant Beaumont crossed the road to retrieve another message from one of the shops opposite the post office. When no one came by 3.00pm, Mr Beaumont left, despondent.

The newsmen drifted away to a nearby pub, where they came face to face with 'Tonner' Swaine and Grant Beaumont. As Bert Stansbury later recounted to author Alan Dower: "'Tonner" looks at us and goes white – dead white – with shock and anger, and he cries out: "What are you bastards doing here?"'

The press were now onto the story and Swaine returned to Adelaide to face Superintendent Lenton. The police tried to suppress news of the 'Dandenong letters' with a curt 'no comment', but Grant and Nancy Beaumont remained in town for several more days. The following day, Grant Beaumont again stood in front of the post office, waiting for the man who would never come. On the third day he shifted to opposite the post office, in front of Patterson's Store, just in case he had made a mistake.

Days later, more letters, written in the same round hand, were posted to Grant and Nancy Beaumont's family home in Somerton Park. One of them was written in red ink.

Dear Mum and Dad,

We had a really beautiful lunch today. We had some turky [sic], and a lot of vegetables. They tasted really nice. The man is feeding us really well. The man took us to see the Sound of Music yesterday. Little Grant fell asleep in it though. He could not understand it. The man was very disappointed that you brought all those policemen with you. He knew all the time that they were there, he says that is why he sent the message to go across the street so that it would disturb the positions of the policemen. The man said that I had better stop now, so I will. Grant and Arnna send you their love.

Love Jane, Arnna and Grant.

x x x x x x x x x x x x x x x x x x x x x x

A second letter, also posted on 29 February, was allegedly from 'the man' himself:

Dear Mr. and Mrs. Beaumont,

I am terribly sorry that I could not hand you your children back to you when you were in Dandenong, but I knew that you had detectives with you, and the main street was so busy.

I am taking extra good care of the kiddies for you. I took little Grant to the doctor because of his gashed knee. He is feeling a lot better now. (Gashed to his ankle).

Actually, in a way, it is your own fault that I did not return them. I saw the letter that Jane wrote before she sent it and it definately [sic] said that there were to be no police (and you know that that includes detectives as well).

I apologize also for all the phone calls at the Post Office, William's and Roger David's, but I had to contact you somehow. Like William's, the Post Office soon became quite "BITCHY". I got frantic when they would not give you any more messages. Then I got into contact with whom I *believe was the Dandenong Post Office master.*

I guess it is too late now, isn't it. I will put them on the train to Adelaide one of these days in the near future, so you had better have their rooms cleaned up!

The assumed Postmaster gave me a phone number to ring. I did so in a hurry. But the girl there lied miserably by saying that a Mr. G. A. Beaumont had not been registered there. If only I could have talked to you then, you might have had your children safely by now!

Isn't it a pitty [sic] you brought those Detectives!

I will write to you as often as possible. I will let Jane and perhaps Arnna write to you.

I am sorry for all the inconvenience I have caused you over the past two and a quarter years (nearly).

Yours faithfully,
"THE MAN"

A third letter, with a faded Dandenong postmark and the date indecipherable, arrived some time later.

Dear Mum and Dad,

I wish you could have got us when you were over here but the man said that you brought some policemen with you. I wish that you had not done that. If you had not, we might have been home by now with you both. The man said that he will let us come home on the train one day. I want you to know and never forget, no matter what happens, that we still love you both very much.

Love,

Jane, Arnna and Grant.

x x x x x x x x x x x x x x x x x x x x x x

Stan Swaine's decision to give credence to a cruel hoax hastened the demise of his police career. He later left SAPOL and became a private investigator, but never gave up hope that he would solve the case. Grant and Nancy Beaumont were badly burned by the incident and decided not to grant any more interviews to the media. They have maintained that stance for more than four decades.

In May 1992, advances in technology solved the mystery of the Dandenong letters. High-tech analysis was able to extract fingerprints from the letters and a 41-year-old Melbourne man was identified and questioned. At first, the man refused to admit to writing the letters, but detectives obtained an example of his teenage handwriting and compared it to the letters sent in 1968. After several days of 'intense negotiation' between Adelaide detectives and the Melbourne man and his solicitor, he confessed to sending the letters to the family when he was 17, as a hoax, and then phoning the Dandenong Post Office to ensure Grant Beaumont stood there all day, waiting for his children to return.

Superintendent Jim Litster informed the media that, 'We are able to confirm the letters were in fact written by the male person [but] were in no way connected with the disappearance of the three children. I understand the person involved is extremely remorseful and it would seem that an act that he had carried out as an immature youth has come back to haunt him.'

Owing to statutes of limitation, no charges were laid against the perpetrator of the hoax.

Chapter 6

Amanda's Story

Stuart met with Amanda Harrison, who had by then reverted to her maiden name, in the middle of 2006. 'I always remember,' Stuart later told me, 'and I've told Amanda this, my initial thoughts were that she was not exactly what I expected. She sounded very young on the phone, but she was in her 60s and was a very mature woman.

'We didn't start off straight away talking about Warwick; I just wanted to get to know her first and get her to relax. I took a liking to her straight away. I could tell that she was a very genuine lady. The way she spoke, she was very clear in what she was saying and fiercely intelligent. She kept on saying during that first conversation, "I don't want you to think that I'm a crackpot, this is just what I know."' They talked for two hours.

Stuart had gathered a lot of information about Hank, and he wanted to see if Amanda's story matched what he had uncovered in Adelaide. 'I took into consideration that Amanda had read the book on the Beaumont children and she could have used that in making up a story,' Stuart explained later. 'But I had been to Glenelg and Hank did live close to the beach; he was a successful businessman with wealth and position, and he had allegedly sexually abused his son and got away with it. He was already starting to tick a lot of boxes.'

Amanda told Stuart she had met Warwick in 1990, when he was 40. 'He had a real presence,' she said. 'I'd never met anyone like him. We just talked and talked ...'

'I know he loved me, but he was just so mercurial ... up one day, down the next. Even after we separated, he would contact me and we would get together. He'd be pleased to see me one day, and then sad or exhausted the next. One week I was *persona non grata*, and then I was "the witch" and he'd scream at me to get out of his life.'

Warwick was already an alcoholic with one failed marriage behind him when they met. 'He's had several breakdowns over the years and was addicted to prescription medicine after suffering a back injury in a car accident,' Amanda said. 'He had been committed to a hospital a couple of times, as he was in the first year of our marriage. But at no point was he diagnosed as psychotic ... and what he was saying about his father abusing him was absolutely true.'

Warwick told Amanda that his father was a heavy drinker at home. 'As a boy, when Hank was drunk, Warwick hid in a large cupboard among the pots and pans so he wouldn't cop a beating ... or worse.' She admitted that she did not get on with her father-in-law herself, and was not impressed by his wealth or power over the family. She could see right through his veneer of respectability, she said. She described Hank as 'tall, grey-haired and tanned' but with 'dead eyes'; he was also 'intelligent, cunning, persuasive and manipulative.'

While Amanda was married to Warwick, she noticed he would fall into a deep sleep at night, and she would often find him face down on his pillow, having difficulty breathing. It was later explained to her by a psychologist that Warwick might have been reliving his sexual abuse as a child, as if he had the weight of his father pressing down on him. Warwick told her that when he heard his father 'swishing in the hallway', dressed in his silk pyjamas, he would lie face down and pretend to be asleep. It rarely stopped him from being attacked.

Stuart asked Amanda about Warwick's grandmother, who also lived in the family home. She was a strict presence in the house, Amanda said. 'Warwick's grandmother was often left in charge of him when he was young,' Amanda said. 'She was a very evil woman ... she made Warwick eat her faeces; she had this special blue chamber pot she kept under her bed and fed him from that.'

Warwick once made the following remark to Amanda about his grandmother: 'You don't know the half of it ... it is too painful to talk about.'

Amanda said Anya, Warwick's mother, knew what was happening to Warwick when he was a boy, but did nothing about it. 'Family members told me that Warwick's mother would never allow other children to stay there overnight. What does that say about her?' She pointed out. '[Anya's] sister told me that Anya had been sexually abused by her own father – a drunken Irish policeman – which didn't surprise me.

'Anya's sisters said she protected them from their father, but some victims rationalise their own abuse. Anya may have thought she was okay, so Warwick would be as well. He wasn't. Warwick told me many things about his abusive childhood, but he also said his father did other things to him that were too horrible to talk about.'

Stuart asked about guns in the house – was Warwick scared of his father in that respect? Amanda said that Hank had a fascination with guns, and had a safe in the cellar where he kept them, but that Warwick was just as scared of Hank's power and influence.

'Warwick said Hank threatened to put him in a mental home and throw away the key,' she remembered. 'He said Hank had the power to do that. When he was in hospital after his nervous breakdown, the staff stopped the phone calls from his parents because they were making him worse. Warwick was told by a psychiatrist not to have anything to do with them. Hank later rang Warwick and said he was "killing his mother" (she had bowel cancer at the time) with his attitude and, before we knew it, they were back in our lives.'

After Warwick's mother died in 1994, Hank's health declined and he ended up marrying his housekeeper, Norma. Amanda confirmed that Warwick believed he would inherit his father's estate, and was upset that Norma received the bulk of the money. 'Warwick hated money but he loved what you could do with it,' Amanda said. 'Hank paid him enough money to go away and live independently, but after our marriage ended and Warwick was a recovering alcoholic, his money was put into a trust and administered by the public trustee.'

Warwick thought that he could get money out of Norma by threatening to go to the media about his sexual abuse. 'Norma actually rang me and asked if "rumours" that Hank abused his son were true. She had heard this from other people, including family, and was very concerned about it all. She also knew about Hank's satin fetish and his dressing up. Warwick told me he was threatened that if he said anything, he would be institutionalised, and that's when he really went downhill. Warwick was under no illusion about the power of the people Hank mixed with.'

Stuart agreed that Hank had obviously been a powerful figure in Glenelg, but questioned how he'd remained so anonymous. 'Hank was like wallpaper,' Amanda explained. 'He just fit in; he was a local, and people of his social standing don't abduct children from the beach. No one would have suspected Hank, even if the kids had hopped in his car out the front of the pie shop.' And if the children did walk to Hank's home after buying their pies and pasties with a £1 note, laneways either side of the family home provided cover. 'Even today, you never see a soul walking up those laneways, because they lead nowhere,' Amanda added. Having walked the lanes himself, Stuart had to agree with her.

After their marriage ended, Warwick slipped back into alcohol and prescription drug abuse, although Amanda still encouraged him to continue his counselling. 'Some people are too frightened to even go back and confront the memory of what happened,' Amanda told Stuart. 'I reassured him, "If you survived the event, you'll survive the memory." I was told I was just a nurse and what did I know? Part of the reason Warwick was afraid, he told me, was because if he faced up to everything that happened in that house, he could lose his mind completely.'

Stuart wanted to know – what did Amanda want us to do with the information she was sharing? Any story about what might have happened to the Beaumont children always had a huge impact in the media, who had a habit of running away with the story and turning it into something else, so it was important for us to verify what she was saying. Going public with this information was also bound to affect Warwick's health and his family.

'The difficult thing is that none of the family will back me,' Amanda said. 'That includes Warwick. It makes me nervous that I could be portrayed as a bitter and twisted ex-wife who thought she had access to the family's money – millions of dollars – and didn't get it. Even when I first met Warwick, the talk was all about me being interested in their money. I saw how the rest of the family operated around money and that just wasn't me. I didn't want anything to do with them. They, in turn, wanted nothing to do with Warwick when he had his mental breakdown. I told them he may never recover from his illness, and they replied, "We can't help you, dear, we just bought a new holiday house."

'But the truth should win out,' Amanda continued. 'Mr and Mrs Beaumont deserve to know what happened to their children. I believe Hank may have been a member of a paedophile ring and there are other people involved and there are other victims.'

It was a common enough theory, Stuart acknowledged, that there had been a paedophile ring operating in Adelaide at the time, but it was incredibly hard to prove.

Stuart asked Amanda if it would be worthwhile for him to talk to her ex-husband about what he knew, but Amanda had no idea what shape Warwick was in. 'If by some miracle he's not drinking or abusing his medication, and he has been eating well and he's physically well – and I don't think he would be getting any counselling at the moment – it's a possibility.

'But be careful,' she warned. 'Warwick wouldn't make a good witness in a court of law, because they would bring up all his mental issues and make him look like a fool. He's very fragile, and I don't think he would be able to hold up under the scrutiny. Even a court of law can't force someone to talk about something if they don't want to. For some people, it is just too painful to remember.'

Amanda had not spoken to Warwick since he phoned some years before, to say that his father had passed away. She gave Stuart the names of some people he could talk to from the extended Harrison family, and friends in close proximity to the family who could corroborate what she was saying, especially about Hank's satin fetish.

Stuart promised to keep in touch, and met with Amanda many times over the next six months, ensuring that her story never changed after that first meeting – and it didn't. He also completed a number of reference checks regarding Amanda's work history, which supported his opinion that she was telling the truth about her ex-husband and his family. Her former employers, two of whom were the heads of leading correctional centres, provided exemplary references, among the most glowing he had ever read. Words such as 'honest, reliable, trustworthy, intelligent, experienced and caring' peppered the references, which ended with a recommendation to 'hire without hesitation'.

Stuart contacted Amanda's sister in Victoria, who had spent 20 years in the police force. 'I needed to know if Amanda might have an axe to grind regarding Warwick and the family,' he explained to me. Her sister revealed that Amanda wanted nothing to do with the family while she was in a relationship with Warwick, let alone now they were divorced. Amanda had also shared her concerns about her father-in-law with her sister from the very start, having felt immediately that his outwardly confident public persona masked an abusive, deviant personality in private.

When Amanda had read *Searching for the Beaumont Children*, she told her sister what Warwick had once said about his father and the Beaumonts. Amanda's sister advised her either to go to the police or contact the author.

Amanda contacted the author.

Chapter 7

Clairvoyants and Charlatans

Over the years, the Beaumont investigation has often defied logic. For five decades, the case has been open season for spiritualists, clairvoyants, pendulum swingers, vision-seekers, hypnotists, religious fanatics, scatter-brained theorists and plain cranks, each having come up with their own solutions to the mystery. These people pestered the parents, the police and members of the press. As one journalist later noted, the Beaumont parents 'suffered these people – many of them fools – perhaps not gladly, but certainly not impatiently'. But then, they had little choice but to listen; who knew what was fake and what was genuine?

In the most high-profile example of spiritualist 'interference', there is no doubt that Gerard Croiset's entry into the case in mid-1966 reignited public interest in the investigation when it had badly stalled. The involvement of the clairvoyant, however, ultimately did nothing but cast a shadow over the unsolved case.

A printer named Jan Van Schie, who worked at the *Adelaide Advertiser*, had written to the Dutch clairvoyant to ask if he could help solve the mystery. Van Schie showed Croiset's reply to the editor of the *Advertiser*, who published the clairvoyant's 'visions' in early August 1966. According to the *Advertiser*, Gerard Croiset believed the children were buried 'about half a mile from where they were last seen'.

The clairvoyant asked that photographs and news film of the Glenelg beachfront be sent to him, so that he could pinpoint where the children were buried. Brighton businessman Barry Blackwell, who had already contributed $2,000 towards the reward, tried to charter a helicopter to film the Glenelg area. 'I really don't believe in this sort of thing,' Blackwell confided to the press, 'but I am told that Mr Croiset has had uncanny success in finding missing children.'

John Kroeger, the editor of *The News* in Adelaide, instructed his London correspondent, Jules Zanetti, to fly immediately to Holland with photos of the Glenelg area, to interview the clairvoyant. In the interview, Croiset said, 'I see an overhanging rock plateau under which there are stones of a nice colour and behind is a cave or hollow.' This claim, reported in *The News* on 3 August, resulted in hundreds of people flocking to Glenelg Beach, looking for any evidence of the missing children.

That night, Australian newscaster Brian Taylor spoke to Gerard Croiset via radio-telephone, live on television. With the help of an interpreter, Taylor had a long conversation with Croiset, having tracked him down at his holiday home in Zandvoort, Holland. Croiset told Taylor that he had been working on the disappearance of the children 'for some time now'. The clairvoyant asked for a detailed map of the local area, but begged off being asked more questions, because 'the faint (telephone) line was making him tired and interfering with his ability as a clairvoyant'.

A Channel 7 cameraman filmed the stretch of beachfront from Port Stanvac to West Beach from a Cessna aircraft, chartered by the television network. Brian Taylor was on board; he sent the film, some recent photographs of the three children and some background information to Croiset in early August. After viewing the material, Croiset said the children 'lie buried in sand two kilometres [about 1¼ miles] from where they were last seen at Glenelg'. He also concluded that the man seen with the children on Colley Reserve had nothing to do with their disappearance. 'They crawl through a little hole,' Croiset told him. 'Suddenly the whole lot tumbles down – instantly. I cannot see if it is water or sand. They crawl towards the end of the hole and suddenly I don't see them any more.'

Despite the fact that the police had searched local drains the day after the children disappeared, volunteers, armed with a fire hose, now tried to flush out rubbish from a stormwater drain at the south end of Glenelg Beach. The first drain was clear but the second was blocked with rocks and sand. The Glenelg Fire Brigade lent a hose to wash about 30 feet of sand from the drain, which had been caused by recent storms and high tides. Nancy Beaumont was 'pleased' that the search was still going on. She had always felt the children could have met with an accident, and if they were dead, she prayed their death had 'been quick' and that they had not been kidnapped.

Supporters decided to bring Gerard Croiset to Australia. The airfare was about $1,200, so company director and successful Adelaide real estate agent Con Polites became involved. Polites, the city's biggest landlord, was known for stamping his buildings with the family name in large blue and white boxes (the Greek national colours), which lit up at night all over Adelaide. Known for the limousine in which he was typically driven, as well as a large, white moustache, Polites sponsored Croiset's visit to Australia and became the clairvoyant's chief advocate for the next thirty years.

Croiset became interested in one theory in particular. In August 1966, a Brighton undertaker reported that a century-old crypt on the beachfront, near the Minda Home for the handicapped, had been demolished in 1954. Eight bodies were removed from the crypt before it was filled in with rubble and buried by sand. Could the Beaumont children have walked up the Esplanade from Glenelg and crawled into one of the openings to the crypt? An intensive search of the area was conducted and no trace of the children – or any crypt – was found. But the 'Minda' reference raised a darker doubt in the minds of many people living in Adelaide. Could one of the patients have kidnapped the Beaumont children as they walked home that hot afternoon, and buried their bodies on the sandy foreshore in front of the Minda home?

It was a fear largely born out of ignorance about the handicapped, but Douglas Buxton Hendrickson, a doctor who worked at Minda, promoted the theory that the Beaumont children could have met their deaths on the hospital grounds. In September 1966, he contacted Gerard Croiset and informed him that he, his 14-year-old son and another member of staff had spent much of the previous month scouring the foreshore at the front of the complex. They had found three items – a battered straw hat, the remains of a dead bird and a piece of black material. Could these be related to the missing Beaumonts? Croiset told Hendrickson he should continue digging within 'half a metre' of where the straw hat was found.

In the interim, however, maintenance staff had dumped tonnes of soil in the area, to stop the edge of the grounds being eroded by sand and wind. Although Mr Lennon, the Minda superintendent, wanted Hendrickson to stop digging on the site, the new developments meant a more coordinated approach had to be undertaken. Front-end loaders were used to remove tonnes of soil and sand, but nothing of interest was found. A Channel 7 cameraman filmed the excavation and photographed the area, so that images could be sent to Croiset in Holland.

Croiset replied that his instructions had been misunderstood … he had meant '14 to 16-and-a-half metres' from where the straw hat was discovered. Searchers should look for a 'kinderwagon' (a child's pram) as a marker. Soon after this clue was reported, a child's pram was found in a thicket by a 21-year-old patient – but it was quickly established that the young patient had planted the pram because he 'wanted to help'.

Dr Hendrickson led a group of volunteers in shifting tonnes of rubble and sand. For several hours, the group followed what appeared to be 'a tunnel'. Hendrickson's group found the bones of some sheep, articles of rotting clothing and an old purse, but nothing related to the children. The Minda superintendent finally forced Hendrickson to sign a document that he would stop digging on the hospital grounds and limit his involvement to areas sanctioned by investigating police. Hendrickson, who now believed firmly in his own psychic ability, refused to sign the letter and withdrew from the formal search altogether.

Gerard Croiset arrived in Adelaide from the Netherlands, via Singapore and Sydney, on the night of 8 November 1966. He was travelling with interpreter Gary Smeding, a Dutch-born cabinetmaker whom Con Polites had arranged to escort Croiset to Adelaide, and who thought he knew the area the clairvoyant was describing. Croiset told pressmen he 'saw' the children buried under a block of flats, but later changed his story a number of times.

There was no media presence at Sydney Airport when the pair departed for Adelaide, but it was a different story when Croiset arrived. On the tarmac, hundreds of people tried to talk to the clairvoyant; others wanted to shake his hand, or tried to give him notes and letters. The Dutchman, with 'magnetic hazel eyes, chiseled artistic profile and a thick mop of halo-like, auburn hair' was then driven by Con Polites' driver to 'a secret location', before starting work on the search the next day.

When first contacted about the disappearance of the three Beaumont children, Gerard Croiset stated, 'There was no foul play, nor were they kidnapped. The children are dead. I am almost certain they suffocated; smothered alive. There was some sort of collapse.'

Adelaide police, who had no previous experience or success with clairvoyants, viewed Croiset as 'just another searcher'. Glenelg's Detective Sergeant 'Wings' Blight put the situation in Adelaide into perspective thus: 'Naturally we hope that he finds the children and we're prepared to appeal to the public to give him a fair go, but we aren't particularly hopeful. From what I have seen on the correspondence with Croiset and what has been published about his theories, I feel he has no idea of the size and nature of the country. He has no idea of the distances involved and all the sandhills to be searched if we are to follow his directions. ... If Croiset finds the Beaumont children it will be sheer luck ...'

During his lifetime, Gerard Croiset was variously known as 'The Wizard of Utrecht', 'The Dutchman with the X-Ray Eyes', 'The Miracle Man of Holland', 'The Man Who Mystifies Europe' and 'Croiset the Clairvoyant'. According to his 1964 biography, Croiset did not accept financial reward for his work and paid his own expenses when investigating a murder or missing person case. He first made himself known to Dutch police when he offered to assist them in the case of a murdered girl in 1949. Handed a sealed box, Croiset correctly revealed its contents as being a blood-stained shoe belonging to the dead girl, 'unknown' details of the crime scene and even the name of the murderer. The truth was, however, that Croiset had access to confidential police information about certain crimes, which appeared to have helped him in his 'predictions'.

Croiset would use a very simple ploy when investigating missing people. He would say the body was 'under the ground' or 'in the water' and that their bodies would be found within six days. He knew that it took several days for a submerged body to float to the surface; if someone had gone missing near water, there was a good chance that the body would eventually be found. If he said a body was buried, it was unlikely ever to be recovered and no one could prove he was wrong.

Croiset started his first search day in Adelaide at 10.00am, at the spot on Colley Reserve where the Beaumont children were last seen. The clairvoyant walked two miles southward along the Glenelg beachfront, while Con Polites, Barry Blackwell, Dr Douglas Hendrickson and a large press contingent followed. He was then driven through the streets of Glenelg, and when he went into Moseley Street, where the children went missing, the clairvoyant got out of the car and leant up against the wall of one of the shops, to gather 'vibrations' of the children's last movements.

Croiset and his entourage drove past the Beaumonts' Harding Street home, without stopping, until they came to the Minda Home in nearby King George Avenue. 'It is where I saw the children under the sand in a vision,' Croiset said. The clairvoyant stated that he had 'a very strong feeling' that the children's remains were buried there, but it was now five o'clock in the afternoon and the search ended for the day.

The following day, Croiset was driven around Adelaide, looking for the area he had seen in his 'visions', but complained that he could not pinpoint where the children's bodies were because there were too many people following him. The Dutch clairvoyant was 'exhausted' and suddenly announced that he would be leaving Australia the next day.

That night, however, Con Polites was contacted by a Mrs Goldworthy from the nearby suburb of Paringa Park, not far from where Jane and Arnna Beaumont had attended primary school. The woman told Polites that the Beaumonts often played with neighbouring children on a vacant block next to a warehouse at the end of the street. The warehouse had previously been used as a brick pit and it was possible that one of the 'chutes' leading to the long-demolished brick kiln still existed. Could the children have crawled into one of the chutes, she wondered, been buried in a cave-in, and their bodies entombed in concrete when the warehouse floor was completed the previous September?

In a hastily organised press conference at the Hotel Australia, on Friday 11 November, Croiset said the children were not buried at Minda after all. Instead, Croiset now believed the bodies of the children were buried 8 to 10 feet underground in 'a bunker' or 'well' under a local warehouse.

This new 'revelation' caused a national sensation. After originally wanting to have nothing to do with Croiset's visit, Mr and Mrs Beaumont changed their minds and asked for the Dutch clairvoyant to visit the family home before he left Adelaide. The day he visited them held a special significance for the family – 11 November would have been the eighth birthday of their second child, Arnna. The meeting, which lasted only 15 minutes, ended amicably, with the parents 'very relieved' that Croiset did not find anything. They even bought Croiset a 'going away' gift – a writing case covered in kangaroo skin.

Mr H. F. Saint, the part-owner of the grocery warehouse Croiset had pinpointed, said that when the building was completed the previous September, the disused brick chutes and kiln had been checked thoroughly before being filled in with rubble and concreted over. A throng of local media followed Croiset inside the 4,000-square-foot warehouse, and found it filled with rows and rows of cardboard boxes. Croiset, who had been to the warehouse earlier that morning, took Detectives Zeunert and O'Brien to the northwest corner of the floor. Walking directly to a point about eight feet from the north wall of the warehouse, Croiset pointed to the floor and stated definitively, 'This is where they are buried.'

Croiset later qualified his claims, saying that the children were within a 40 metre radius of the spot he had pinpointed – effectively the whole warehouse. 'Yesterday, I found them,' he said before he flew out of the country. When asked what needed to happen next, Croiset replied, 'It is up to you. My work is done.'

Gerard Croiset left Australia for relative obscurity, but his infamous connection with the Beaumont case remains. Not that everyone believed in the 'Great Croiset' for the right reasons – Con Polites' driver later told detectives that on the first night Croiset was staying at the Australia Hotel, he gave the Dutchman a local newspaper and said, 'Right ... give me all the winners at Morphettville on Saturday.'

* * *

Other offers of clairvoyant help and insight followed, though they attracted less sensation. A Sydney man named Tom Fear, a self-described 'dreamer', came forward in 1967. Fear, who had worked with police before, allegedly finding the body of a seven-month-old child 'in a dream' and collecting a NSW State Government reward of £1,000 for his services, made his own way to Adelaide and told police that he had 'dreamed' that the Beaumont children were buried in the Adelaide Hills, in an area near the Torrens Gorge. Police told Fear that if he felt the children's remains were up in the hills, he should go and find them. This was a mistake; Fear was found digging up a stretch of bitumen road, but told local police he had 'permission to do so'. He was quietly encouraged to return to Sydney.

Several other 'pendulum swingers' arrived at the Beaumonts' home to try their magic on the parents. One placed a pendulum over a map of Glenelg and studied the way in which it swung to determine where the children's remains were buried. Grant and Nancy refused to see another such person from interstate, who wanted to swing a pendulum over black and white photos of the children to see if it gave off a 'positive or negative reaction' as to whether the children were alive.

A water diviner from New Zealand arrived in Adelaide, stating that he could find the bodies of the children because he had the power to receive vibrations on his divining rod in areas where human bones were buried. After an unsuccessful demonstration of his ability, members of the press dissuaded him from calling on the family.

Grant Beaumont despaired, as people with paranormal beliefs called them relentlessly with their theories. 'The latest to call on us,' he said, in a February 1968 interview, 'was a hypnotist. While he was welcome to call, I told him he was only upsetting us … I've got no time for beliefs in crystal balls, pendulums, the stars, spiritualism … Let them go to the police and tell them.'

Chapter 8

Warwick

Amanda gave Stuart her ex-husband Warwick Harrison's address, and Stuart sent him a copy of *Searching for the Beaumont Children*, by registered post. 'I hadn't heard from Warwick so I tried his phone number,' Stuart later recalled, 'but he never answered it. I waited about a month, maybe two months, and I sent him another letter by registered post, and still heard nothing.'

Stuart decided to contact Warwick's adult son, Joel Harrison. He wrote him a letter and sent him *Searching for the Beaumont Children*. 'When I didn't receive a reply from Joel either, I phoned him,' Stuart told me. 'I asked him if he got the book. Joel knew why I wanted to speak to him straight away … He said in a resigned voice, "Mate, I know all about this."'

Warwick's son agreed to meet Stuart at his home. 'When I met him, I said that some people had told me his grandfather Hank may have been involved in the disappearance of the Beaumont children,' Stuart recounted. 'I mentioned his satin fetish and that Warwick had told others he had been abused.' Joel Harrison, a tall young man in his early 30s, said he had known about this for years. His father had previously maintained that he saw the Beaumont children in the backyard of the family home, that summer's day in 1966 when they disappeared.

'I was not surprised,' Joel continued. 'I used to live at the house and my grandfather was completely evil.'

The physical description Joel provided of Hank was nearly identical to that of the chief suspect in the case – a man with a tall, thin face, high forehead and wavy hair – but then, he could have read that in the Beaumont book. Joel spent several years living with his grandparents after his parents' marriage broke up, but now had only intermittent contact with his extended family. Stuart found it interesting that Warwick's son knew his father was abused, while his mother, Warwick's first wife, hadn't known anything about it. 'We confided in one another,' the son said.

Joel repeated the story about Hank wearing satin and swishing down the hallway. 'That was only half of it,' he said. Hank used to make his own 'dresses', he maintained, which covered his body from head to foot – 'Phantom costumes', as Joel described them.

Stuart remembered, 'Joel said he once broke into a room in the adjoining house that nobody was allowed to go in. We knew that there were satin pyjamas and kaftans in there, but Joel said, "There was a *lot* of weird shit in there." He said there were codpieces, frilly stuff, phantom costumes and some "really weird shit". Joel said he "got right stuck into that room and ripped it apart" and that what he found there made him sick.'

Joel also recalled that, when they were in the family pool, Hank would sometimes get a bit too close for comfort and rub up against his grandson. 'Dad tells the story that when he was a boy, Hank would get him to swim between his legs, and he would trap him there underwater until he struggled free. He was a cruel bastard.'

Stuart thought it strange that Warwick would have allowed his son to stay with Hank, given what he alleged had happened to him there. Fortunately, Warwick's son learned tae kwon do from an early age, and was quite proficient at it, but that didn't stop his grandfather from being vindictive. He recounted a story in which he brought a girlfriend over and Hank afterwards put a gun to his head. Stuart thought that was a little bit far-fetched, but the more people he spoke to about Hank, the more he learned about the family patriarch's obsession with guns. 'He loved brandishing them at home,' Joel confirmed.

'It was hell living in that house and I couldn't wait to get out,' Joel went on. Once, the boy made the mistake of touching Hank's 27-foot boat. 'Don't touch my fucking boat, you little c***,' was his grandfather's response. Hank used to tell his grandson, especially on Saturdays, to 'fuck off, you little bastard'. He would say, 'It's my Saturday,' and the boy would head out to the sideshows at Glenelg, as his father had done a generation before him.

Stuart finally asked if he could help set up a meeting with his father. Their relationship was volatile, Joel said, but he agreed to contact Warwick. When Joel told his father he had a book on the Beaumont children in his hands, though, Warwick 'went off'; he had to race over to his father's house to calm him down. For whatever reason, Joel recorded the conversation he had with his father on his iPhone, and later played it to Stuart.

'When they met in the garage, Warwick was upset and yelling, "I knew this day would come,"' Stuart told me. 'Joel was saying, "Dad, you need to tell your story."'

Stuart eventually met Warwick in his modest apartment in Queensland, in October 2007. A tall, well-spoken man greeted Stuart at the door, apologising that he might not be at his best because he was 'sort of in a bit of rehab'.

'I'm a bit of a mess,' Warwick told Stuart.

Warwick took great pains to speak very clearly, very precisely. 'Warwick was very much on the ball when we first met,' Stuart recalled. 'He was upfront, saying, "Mate, I've gone through a fair bit, but at least I'm not on the piss anymore." As he talked, he was "in the moment" and that's what made what he was saying so believable. There was no "um-ing" and "ah-ing" … he was very much to the point.'

They sat down and spoke for almost two hours at that first meeting. 'Warwick was a lovely guy to talk to at that time,' Stuart said. 'He was very clear when he went through his sexual abuse issues. I told him he didn't have to go into it too deeply and he said, "No, it's no problem, I want to talk about it."'

Warwick's mother had been an Irish Catholic and his father a strong Anglican, he began. 'It was a very unhappy marriage … there was some strong bitterness in the family over church beliefs. When my mother died, Hank remarried. My father was too inept to care for himself and needed a carer in later life, as much as he needed a wife. He died of Alzheimer's disease and kidney failure about four or five years ago.'

Warwick then recounted what Amanda had initially told Stuart about Hank … lying in bed and listening to his dad coming down the hallway, and the swish, swish, swish of the satin. He said he knew what was going to happen and that his father had sodomised him at least three times a week for the best part of ten years, until he was big enough and old enough to stand up to him.

Said Stuart: 'He was able to remember everything and as he spoke, it was as if he was there, in the backyard of the family home again. My only regret, and I was jotting all of it down as he was speaking to me, was not recording the conversation. We could have used it as an "on the record" interview, which could have been played to other people … health professionals, the police.'

Warwick said he would go down to the breakfast table in the morning, after the night's abuse, and everything would be normal. 'He couldn't understand it,' Stuart said. 'In the morning, his father acted as if nothing had happened and yet Warwick had been abused the night before. Everything appeared normal, and that confused him. It confused him a lot.'

Warwick also said that Saturday was his father's day for 'dressing up'; he would give him a £1 note and tell him to 'fuck off' for the day. 'His mother, Anya, would play tennis with friends at a private tennis court. Warwick told me the address. I went down there later and it checked it out,' Stuart told me.

'We were paid to go down the sideshows all the time,' Warwick said. 'You could ask for a quid, you could ask for five pound, you could ask for twenty pound … Anything you wanted, as much as you wanted. He always had plenty of money and he coveted his own privacy … for anyone to interrupt his privacy – $10,000 wouldn't buy it back. He'd later say, "I'm so ashamed for what I've done," but he wouldn't go into it in detail.'

Warwick told Stuart about the satin dresses his father made and the pyjamas he wore. 'Hank had no shame,' said Warwick. 'When he wore satin pyjamas, he would masturbate, and you could see the stains on the satin. He kept his dresses in the attic and cellar, in his "special room" in the house next door, and in other houses all over the city.

'You kept walking if you caught him hanging out dresses on the line, or ironing them, or stitching them together,' Warwick went on. 'I know he hated himself for it and he hated what he was doing, but he couldn't stop doing it. He was just a mass of contradictions.'

After an hour of talking, Stuart felt he had developed a good enough rapport with Warwick to ask about the Beaumonts.

'Do you remember the day the kids went missing, the Beaumont kids, on Australia Day 1966?' he asked.

'It was hot,' Warwick said, straight away. 'It was a real bastard of a day … it must have been 40-something plus.' He was in his late teens at the time, working part-time at the local bowling alley. 'When I got home, Mum had gone to tennis. Dad's car was parked in the driveway.' Warwick said he was with some friends, 'smoking ciggies' in the cubby-house, when he saw three children come into the backyard.

Warwick didn't know if his friends saw the children that day, but he did. He said they looked lost. He described the children as having short, cropped hair, and originally thought they were all girls. It wasn't until much later that he found out one of the missing children was a boy. 'The oldest one had a shoulder bag, a type of carry bag,' he said.

The three children went inside the house, but Warwick didn't see them come out. He did, however, see Hank load up the boot of the car with four large bags a little while later. Warwick knew immediately what was in them. 'Hank had sublet one of the houses on the factory grounds to a surfboard manufacturer,' Warwick said. 'He used the plastic surfboard cases to transport his satin dresses around the city, so no one knew what he was doing.'

Hank drove out, but Warwick did not see the children get into the car.

Stuart asked what Warwick thought happened to the children. Warwick said that when the children went inside the house, he'd heard a loud bang, which he initially thought was a gun blast, but then realised was only the front door slamming. Warwick went inside the house himself shortly afterwards. He thought the children must have gone out the front door, because it had been left open and there was no sign of them or his father. He assumed the children met up with his father in the car, at the side of the house.

'What then?' Stuart pressed.

All Warwick would say was, 'They're in the sandpit.'

Stuart could see Warwick was exhausted. But he did ask one more question, arguably the most important question of the interview. Was Warwick saying these things to get back at his father?

'Good question,' Warwick said, 'but no. He was a violent man and a bastard for what he did. You didn't know him.'

Sometime later, Joel explained to Stuart that his father was referring to the sandpit at the family factory – he had told his son as much previously – but speculated that Warwick knew more about it than he was saying. 'Warwick's son said he knows his father better than anybody,' Stuart remembered. 'Joel thinks something else happened, but Warwick isn't telling anyone and he won't discuss it.' Amanda even said Warwick was hiding something, and others involved in the investigation believed the same thing. But what?

'Warwick said he would "swear on the Bible" he saw those children that day,' Stuart later told me. Perhaps one day Warwick would have to – but within weeks, he was in no condition to swear to anything. He entered a downward spiral of prescription drug and alcohol abuse.

Stuart and I passed all this information on to SAPOL – they had professionals who would know how to deal with someone like Warwick, we figured, someone who was damaged by sexual abuse and hell-bent on self-destruction. They would take a statement from Warwick and act upon it. We were sure of it.

Chapter 9

The Warehouse

Constantine Polites was born in 1919, at Port Pirie in South Australia, to Greek farming parents. He grew up in poverty, left school at 16, and moved to Adelaide to work as a general hand at Woolworths in Rundle Street. At age 19, he started a delicatessen business at Port Pirie, having borrowed £100 from his father, before moving back to Adelaide, where he started a phenomenal business career that would eventually make him a multimillionaire. He grew his distinctive moustache on a £1 bet; he won the pound and kept the moustache all his life.

Polites moved to Sydney in the late 1940s and lived there for five years. He married, returned to Adelaide and made his first real estate purchase in 1950, on the Anzac Highway. He bought a building, which became his home and office, and from which he ran a wedding business, before launching a highly successful real estate company. Known as the 'King of Hindley Street', it was said that Polites made a killing in the property boom of the 1960s and 1970s, when he famously 'bought and sold a building a day'. Polites once told a journalist that he had no interests, no hobbies, and no pastimes – only work.

When he bought a building, he would erect a large blue and white sign (the Greek national colours) reading 'POLITES'. He told the

Advertiser in 1993 that he 'always wanted to have his name up in lights' but that it had nothing to do with ego. It was more to do with a feeling of satisfaction that he had achieved success. 'I feel proud that I have achieved these things,' he said. 'It was a medal to myself … you've done a good job.'

In the 1980s, 'King Con' Polites was on *BRW*'s Rich List, with an estimated personal wealth of more than $40 million dollars. Not bad for the son of a Greek immigrant who once declared he could 'spot a conman at 10 paces', never read a book in his life, didn't trust accountants and lived in a large white and blue mansion by the sea, which he named 'The White House', when he wasn't being chauffeured around Adelaide in one of his five Rolls Royces. He also enjoyed thumbing his nose at the Adelaide establishment – he had come from nothing, and had accumulated more wealth than most of his detractors among the upper classes.

But Con Polites, the hard-nosed businessman who built an empire, appeared to have a soft spot when it came to the missing Beaumont children, the 'visions' of Gerard Croiset and a nondescript warehouse at Paringa Park, where, for more than forty years, it was thought the remains of the three children might lie buried.

* * *

It seems clear now, almost fifty years after the fact, that Dutch clairvoyant Gerard Croiset nominated the Paringa Park warehouse as the final 'resting ground' of the three Beaumont children in 1966 because he had no idea where the children were buried, and knew that a building would not be entirely demolished to prove him wrong. But the partial excavation of the warehouse in later years, undertaken by a series of well-meaning people over four decades, became a symbol of the unresolved investigation, and the futility of one man's crusade to prove the doubters wrong.

Although there was no evidence to substantiate Gerard Croiset's November 1966 claim that the Beaumont children were buried there, the warehouse theory quickly took on a life of its own. The Dutchman backed a plan to excavate the concrete floor of the warehouse and later gave the following account of what he 'saw' at the warehouse.

'When I came to the storeroom [warehouse] I got a very strong positive reaction,' Croiset began. 'They [the children] were looking for shelter near friends because it was dark. They were afraid to go home in the dark ... I never thought the children were murdered ... they were looking for shelter. They were huddling behind a fence on some planks and the planks caved in. All this time I had been looking for rocks, but I realised I was looking for concrete.'

On 14 November 1966 – just one week after Gerard Croiset left the country following his sensational claim – the South Australian State Government met to decide whether to finance the excavation of the site, to end the matter once and for all. Cabinet ministers were briefed by police, who had been able to determine the history of the site, locate the original building plans, and interview those people who were responsible for renovating the concrete floor, in work that had commenced the previous August.

Con Polites was quoted in the *Advertiser* the following morning saying, 'I am convinced the children are there. I will be very disappointed if the work of the very dedicated Mr Croiset is not supported by the Government.' But police investigations, the parents of the missing children and, finally, the State Government, did not support Polites' views.

Investigations determined that the warehouse was built in 1955 by the Paringa Press Brick Company. Part of the site's infrastructure included two steel-lined sandpits (10 by 11 by 8 feet deep) and an 'L-shaped' concrete chute, with steps leading down to a depth of about nine feet, for the conveyance of bricks. Another pit, some six feet away, housed the brick conveyance machine, which had a small excavation, of about four by two feet, underneath it. The only other pits on the site were a large, concrete-lined motor pit (3 by 12 by 6 feet deep) and a water soakage pit (4 by 4 by 3 feet deep). Five steam kilns, situated at the rear of the premises, had been built on a concrete floor at ground level. There were no tunnels leading to the kilns.

The brickworks had fallen into disrepair between 1961 and June 1965, when the building was jointly bought by the Western Joinery and Screenings Ltd. The premises were used to store furniture until the renovations began in August 1966. Mr Saint and Mr Starr, co-directors of the company, had regularly visited the site in the previous year – including at the time the Beaumont children went missing – and noticed nothing untoward. In August, the remains of the brickworks were demolished; this included the excavation and filling-in of all pits on the site. Lastly, the floor of the warehouse was put down to a depth of four inches and the single building warehouse was constructed.

On 15 November 1966, State Cabinet declined to authorise excavation work at the Paringa Park warehouse. Announcing the decision, South Australian Premier Mr Walsh stated that a police investigation had shown 'conclusively' that there was no possibility the children had been buried there. Any excavation would be 'a waste of time, money and effort'. It was impossible for the children to have crawled into one of the excavations – or for their bodies to have been hidden there – because of the removal of the steel-lined superstructure and the inspection of excavated pits before concreting. Mr R. L. Golding, the original builder of the brickworks, even took pressmen to the warehouse to show them where the brick pits originally were, and how they had been filled in. 'It would have been impossible for the bodies to have been in the pits from the time the Beaumont children disappeared until the rebuilding, without their having been discovered,' Mr Golding said. There was no 'cave-in'.

Grant Beaumont supported the Government's decision and reconfirmed his confidence in SAPOL. 'If they decided not to dig, then that is fine by me. I have more faith in the police than I do in Mr Croiset and I go along with the police here.'

Others, however, were not so sure. 'I would like to see a vote taken of the people on this,' Con Polites told journalists. 'I feel sure they would be in favour of Mr Croiset's decision.'

A Citizen's Action Committee, which had been formed to investigate the excavation of the warehouse and to raise funds from public donations, was 'flooded' with offers of help. Mr Saint, the owner of the warehouse, originally agreed with the Government's decision not to finance a dig, but came under increasing pressure to allow a partial excavation during the summer of 1966–67, leading up to the first anniversary of the children's disappearance. When Con Polites came on board with the committee, he implored Mr Saint to allow the excavation.

On Thursday 26 January, 1967 – one year to the day after the three Beaumont Children went missing from Glenelg Beach – a group met at the Paringa Park warehouse. The excavation would begin on 1 March and last for a maximum of two weeks, but only after the $7,000 cost had been raised. When donations stalled at $3,000, the Committee again approached the State Government to subsidise the excavation, but the Premier once more declined. The Government was satisfied 'beyond doubt' that the children were not buried there and was not prepared to spend public money on an excavation.

A condition of the owner's support for the excavation was that the work would have to be done by professionals, the costs fully audited and the police were to be in attendance. On 1 March 1967, a single brick internal wall measuring 12 by 8 feet was demolished, and a water-cooled diamond-cutting machine started cutting through a section of the four-inch floor, in the northwest corner that Gerard Croiset had identified. The following day, workmen used jackhammers to dig down to a depth of seven feet and excavate one of the former sandpits. On 3 March, the workmen discovered a number of small 'tunnels', and followed them down to a level of 12 feet.

During the next several days, the dig continued, but could not spread outwards beyond the cavity where the concrete floor had been cut. Some rubbish was found at the bottom of one of the holes – paper bags, grease-proof paper, a chocolate wrapper, bottle tops, a shirt cuff, a rotting towel and orange peel – and in the minds of some of the Citizen's Action Committee who watched the excavations, these somehow became pie and pastie bags, part of a beach towel and a little boy's shirt. There was great excitement about these 'finds', but they were soon confirmed to be worthless rubbish – Grant Beaumont didn't even wear a shirt to the beach the day he disappeared.

Post-hole diggers were used to excavate to a depth of 15 feet, but the project was stopped when funds ran out after ten days of digging, with nothing to show for them except a large hole, which quickly filled with water. From his home in the Netherlands, Gerard Croiset implored the Citizen's Action Committee to keep digging.

South Australian Premier Frank Walsh later put the project into some perspective when he said that he 'could not agree at any stage that the warehouse search was a step in the right direction'. He then extended his Government's public sympathy to Mr and Mrs Beaumont for their 'continued anxiety and sorrow'. The lack of success at the Paringa Park warehouse fuelled decades of speculation, the growth of an urban myth and, thirty years later, yet another excavation attempt.

In 1978, the tireless Con Polites called for further excavation of the site. The property developer was in regular contact with clairvoyant Gerard Croiset, via journalist Dick Wordley, and both men never wavered from the belief that the remains of the three Beaumont children were under the concrete floor. Croiset reiterated his claim that the children had been 'smothered' by a cave-in of 'old underground brick kilns' (which building plans showed never existed) and Polites stated that the original excavation had not gone deep enough; he 'felt so sad we got so far and couldn't achieve what we set out to do.'

The owners of the warehouse remained adamant – they would not authorise another excavation and go through a fiasco like that of March 1967 unless there was a court order instructing them to do so. It was not until almost 20 years later that Polites could organise another dig – after first advocating in 1995 that sophisticated sonar equipment should be used to explore under the floor of the warehouse. SAPOL resisted sanctioning a new dig at the site, 'If there was some evidence to strongly suggest they [the children's remains] are there, well, of course we'd be interested,' said Detective Sergeant Brian Swan, who was now in charge of the investigation. 'But at this stage, the warehouse [theory] is not based on any factual evidence at all.'

But Con Polites would not be deterred. In April 1996, he negotiated with the new owner of the warehouse, who had leased the building to a bathroom renovation company. Almost three decades after Croiset first identified the Paringa Park warehouse as the resting place of the missing children, Con Polites financed a second excavation of the warehouse's concrete floor. Without any clear knowledge of where the old brick pits lay, Polites' team planned to drill holes in the concrete and analyse the soil content. Digging began at 7.00am on 1 May, and by 11.00am, nine holes had been dug. By 3.00pm, the digging had stopped and the team had packed up. Although the core samples proved that there were sandpits under the concrete, nothing of the children was found. Despite this, Polites continued with the partial excavation through June and July. Two specially trained Weimaraner sniffer dogs were used to explore the 'tunnels' that had formed from the excavation of rubble. A newspaper from 1958, a piece of clothing and a man's footprint preserved in sand were found, but no evidence of the Beaumont children. Still, the real estate millionaire would not give up. 'I've had a gut feeling since that day he [Croiset] told me they were there,' he told the *Sunday Mail*. The excavations at the Paringa Park warehouse ended in September 1996, again with nothing to show except a 13cm bone, which was analysed and found to belong to an animal.

'I grew to admire Mr Croiset and like him,' Polites told *The Sunday Mail*'s Shane Maguire. 'I had a lot of respect for him and so I believed I would be letting him down if I didn't pursue what he wanted. The old brick kilns were a well-known playing spot for kiddies all those years ago, and I believe the Beaumont children were playing in a pit, it collapsed and buried them.

'I became so frustrated with not being able to do anything that I often said to my wife that if I could one day buy the building, I will pull it down and search properly ... I have three children of my own and I know I would be devastated if one morning I woke up and found they had gone forever. Any person with compassion would have to want to know what happened to Jane, Grant and Arnna ...

'All those years ago, Mr Croiset told me the children weren't the victims of a crime, just a terrible accident. I asked him how much I could pay him ... he said through an interpreter, "You have insulted me. I don't want any money. I've come out here to find the children." Now, how can you not like a man like that?'

'King Con' Polites died in 2001, aged 82. As far as we know, he went to his grave believing that the bodies of the three children were still buried in the Paringa Park warehouse in Wilton Road.

The warehouse was sold and finally demolished in 2007, when what most people already knew was confirmed – there was nothing there.

Chapter 10

The Satin Man

At the end of Stuart's meeting with Warwick Harrison, Warwick confirmed the names of several of his childhood friends who could provide further information about his troubled teenage years. Stuart agreed to follow this up, because he knew, from his own background in the recruitment industry, that someone who was lying wouldn't do normally do this. A prospective candidate might say they were the best resort manager in Australia, Stuart explained to me, but it was easy to check. A couple of phone calls to their references – or simply contacting people in the industry – and you could soon find out if someone was exaggerating the truth.

Stuart had three names to work with – Craig Johns, Bob Peters and Warwick's closest friend, Steve Parker. Warwick was sure Johns and Peters were in the backyard with him the day he saw the Beaumont children in 1966, while Stevens, who was Warwick's age, was closest to the Harrison family of the three.

Craig Johns proved easiest to find – in the White Pages, of all places. Stuart sent Craig a letter and a copy of *Searching for the Beaumont Children*, then contacted him by phone and said he'd like to talk to him about the case. 'Craig said he knew Warwick for many years as a teenager,' Stuart recalled. 'He lived quite close to Warwick and hung out with him for about ten years. He also knew "old Hank" quite well. I asked him if he had read the book, but he said no, he hadn't. He wanted to hear what I had to say first.'

Craig said he 'loved' going around to Warwick's house every now and then, because Hank would need to go down to Victor Harbor, and he would get a ride with Warwick and Bob Peters, another friend. 'Hank would give us a £1 note each,' Craig remembered. 'Do you know how much a £1 note was in those days? When I was a kid, it was a lot of money and you could have a lot of fun on a day out. We'd go down to Victor Harbor for the day and spend it.'

Craig remembered Hank as being 'very generous' with the young kids in the area. 'He loved giving them money, fishing rods, sports stuff, anything ... "Take it, it's yours," he'd say.'

Although Craig didn't think there was anything 'unusual' about Hank at that time, he remembered the Harrisons as a 'dysfunctional family'.

'Hank was a heavy drinker,' he said, 'and I remember the police were called one night when Warwick threatened his father and one of the front windows was shot out.'

Stuart asked Craig to describe Hank as he remembered him in the 1960s. Hank was about six feet tall, he said, a medium build, tanned, with blondish hair, swept back off the forehead. He added that Warwick directed a lot of bitterness and anger at Hank. 'It couldn't have been for lack of anything, as he was always given what he wanted,' said Craig. 'You could say Warwick was spoilt.'

Craig didn't know anything about seeing the missing Beaumont children, but did remember smoking cigarettes in Warwick's backyard. Craig lost contact with Warwick when they left high school, but years later, in the 1980s, they met again at a barbecue. Craig had gone to university and told Warwick he had lived on campus for a couple of years. 'The next thing Warwick asks me was, "Did you get it up the arse like I used to get it up the arse at home?"' Johns told Stuart. 'I was taken aback a bit, and then Warwick told me he had been abused as a child. I couldn't believe it.'

Finding Bob Peters proved a little more difficult. Stuart sent letters to about fifty "Peters, B" saying he would like to discuss Warwick Harrison, and to please give him a call. They were all sent registered post and most of them were returned to sender.

It was about seven months before Stuart was able to get in contact with Bob, via a contact who knew where Bob's brother worked in Adelaide. 'When I was finally able to arrange a meeting with Bob, I said, "I've been trying to track you down for months and all I got was these return to sender notices." He said, "Yeah, I returned several of your letters." When I asked why, he said the Harrisons were a very strange family indeed.'

Bob didn't want to talk much about the Harrisons. 'There was something completely wrong with them,' he said. He confirmed, however, that Hank would give him, Warwick and Craig Johns a £1 note when they went down to Victor Harbor. 'I was only 15 or 16 at the time, but we went because we knew we were going to get some money to spend. I always remember Hank giving us the money and saying, "You guys fuck off." I always found it rather annoying that a father used that sort of language around kids back then.'

Stuart asked Bob to describe Hank. He remembered him as 'well-dressed, tallish, medium build, long face with a large forehead, wavy, light brown hair, brushed back … he looked a little like [convicted child murderer] Bevan von Einem, actually, as I remember von Einem in the media.' That wasn't a helpful comparison, Stuart thought.

Bob had another important snippet of information. Another man often went with Hank on their road trips to Victor Harbor. The man's name was Frank Barsley and he lived with his family in a large two-storey house on the other side of the Anzac Highway. Bob didn't know where Hank and Barsley went once they got to

Victor Harbor, 'but it wasn't the pub,' he laughed; these weren't regular guys with whom you could have a nice chat.

Bob Peters knew nothing about Warwick's alleged sexual abuse, or the disappearance of the Beaumont children. He did remember his father having harsh words with Hank one day, but then, relationships with the Harrisons were often strained.

'I don't want to talk about the family any more,' he then said to Stuart. He then suddenly got up, excused himself and said goodbye.

One name Amanda had given Stuart was Rose Parker, the first wife of Warwick's close friend Steve Parker. Stuart thought it would be good to have a chat with her before he met Steve, so he sent her the book on the Beaumont children, with the message, 'I need to talk to you regarding somebody you know ... you could help.'

Rose was a registered nurse, like Amanda, and Stuart was struck by her professionalism and candour; she was pleasant and very precise. Rose told him she got to know Warwick's family very well when she was married to Steve in the late 1960s and early 1970s. When Stuart told her that Warwick claimed he was abused, she offered, 'I knew there was something wrong with him because he hated his dad from an early age ... Warwick didn't have a kind word to say about him. That [he was abused] makes complete and utter sense.'

Rose said she'd seen evidence of Hank's 'satin fetish' and that he was a 'sexual deviant.' She supported Amanda and said his fetish 'was very well known in close family circles'. You could not wear satin clothes to the house, Rose said, and there was a very strict 'code', because Hank was easily sexually aroused and he 'could not help himself' when he came into contact with satin.

'I knew what was going on underneath those satin garments he wore,' she said, 'and I stopped my children from coming to the house.'

She also confirmed that there was a room in the adjoining

house you were not allowed to go into. 'Hank had two sides to his personality ... one was his public face, which could be very charming, and the other side was a very nasty, vindictive man.'

Stuart found his best rapport with Rose's former husband, Steve Parker. Steve was close to the family and had known Warwick when he was a teenager. Stuart formed a friendship with Steve over the seven years that followed; they met regularly in Adelaide for long discussions about everything from business (both Steve and Stuart run their own businesses) to spirituality and mental health issues. Steve helped Stuart with names and addresses, and provided him with context for some of the information Stuart discovered about the Harrison family.

'Steve was not surprised at all that Warwick may have been sexually abused,' Stuart says. 'He had heard rumours for many years. Steve definitely knew about Hank's satin fetish; that satin "turned him on" greatly, and that he also wore dresses. He knew that Hank was initially raised as a girl – these were well known stories in the inner family circle – and about the private room Hank kept in the house next door. 'By all accounts, nobody was allowed anywhere near that room,' said Steve.

Steve's father worked for the government; the family travelled a lot and lived overseas. Steve could remember his father going to Hank's home one night in the late 1960s, and drunkenly yelling out, 'I know what you did, you bastard.'

Steve also said that on many occasions during the 1960s, either while walking home from school or heading up to the shops at Glenelg, he would see Hank driving around Glenelg in his Pontiac. 'He wasn't dictated to by [office] hours,' Steve said, which might explain why Hank could have been home on Australia Day 1966, a normal working day. 'He seemed to spend a lot of time cruising around town.'

Warwick learnt to drive in an old truck at the factory, Steve remembered, earning the ire of his father when he once rolled a forklift. The factory also had a light-coloured, khaki-green Holden utility with a canopy; it was used by different sections of the company, but mainly by the maintenance shop. When Warwick was about 17 years old, Hank totally rebuilt the car, sprayed it in a different colour, and gave it to his son as a gift when the boy started at Flinders University. This was hardly the 'new car every year' story Brian McHenry had related to Stuart, but it showed that Hank had some affection for his son – or perhaps that he was buying Warwick off.

Stuart also asked Steve to describe Hank as he remembered him. Although Hank would have been middle-aged (in his late forties in 1966), Steve said he had a 'babyish face' and always looked 'younger than his years'. He was tall, fit and tanned, with darkish blond hair, and only seemed to start ageing once he got into his fifties, when his hair turned silver and he put on a bit of weight. As he got older, Hank became 'stooped' – a shadow of the man who swam at Glenelg, played golf and kept himself fit.

Whenever Steve thought of new information that might be helpful, he would call Stuart from Adelaide. Steve was still in regular contact with Warwick, and Stuart was impressed by the fact that Steve was loyal to him, and wanted him to get the best help available.

Stuart spent about six months trying to dig up information about Frank Barsley – the man Bob Peters said had gone to Victor Harbor with Hank – to no avail. But as far as Stuart was concerned, the rumours about Hank weren't rumours anymore. According to a number of people, Hank Harrison was a paedophile, operating within a few hundred metres of Colley Reserve at the time the children went missing, completely undetected. He'd been hiding in plain sight, protected by his wealth and influence, and his family's fear.

In Adelaide in the 1960s, that might have been enough to get away with murder.

* * *

In 2010, Amanda Harrison was working in a correctional centre in Brisbane when she shared a coffee with one of the psychologists on staff. They talked generally, amongst other things, about the rise in sexual and physical abuse, and the immense damage suffered by the victims. The psychologist mentioned one of her former patients, a man in his 50s whom she had been counselling for years, had been sexually and physically abused by his father. He was also made to 'hang out' at Glenelg Beach, as 'bait' to procure other young boys, who were also abused by his father.

Amanda resisted the temptation to tell the psychologist about the parallels with her ex-husband, but now wondered if more than one man had been involved in the Beaumont children's disappearance. She thought it would be a good idea for Stuart to talk to the psychologist to determine if there was any connection to the Beaumont children. After much coaxing, the psychologist agreed to an interview, as long as it would not break her client's confidentiality.

In the end, Stuart spoke to the psychologist for about 40 minutes. He did not say too much about how far he had gone regarding his own research, and no names were mentioned.

The female psychologist said that her patient had lived in the Glenelg area in the 1960s and early 70s, and that his father had sexually and physically abused him, as well as other family members. The father was a tall, physically imposing man. He would make his son go to Glenelg Beach to find children for his dad to molest.

The psychologist went on to say the father had been in prison, though she was not sure for what crime. His now-adult son was a broken man, another soul destroyed through years of torment at the hands of his father.

At the end of the interview, Stuart asked if she believed what her patient had recounted was true. She said, as a trained psychologist, that she did. Stuart also pressed her for the last name of the family, because the information could be very important. Reluctantly, but reasoning that the father or son could not be identified by a surname alone, she agreed.

The name was Barsley – the same name of the tall man who went to Victor Harbor with Hank and the boys in the 1960s.

For more than 12 months, Stuart tried to contact the Barsley family who had lived in Glenelg all those years ago, but without success. They too had disappeared without a trace.

Chapter 11

Other Rooms

On 12 January 1965, the bodies of two schoolgirls were found buried in sand dunes near Cronulla, south of Sydney city. Christine Sharrock and her next-door neighbour Marianne Schmidt, both aged 15, had gone missing the previous day, on a trip to the beach with Marianne's four younger siblings. It was an eerie precursor to what would happen to the Beaumont children the following year. The difference was that the bodies of Christine and Marianne were found – raped, mutilated and buried in a sand dune.

The chief suspect in the Wanda Beach murders was a 16-year-old boy, seen walking into the dunes with the two girls by Marianne's brothers and sister. When the girls did not come back, the four remaining Schmidt children walked back to Cronulla station and caught a train to their West Ryde home. Several 'beach pests' were at Wanda that day, exposing themselves to young people and generally annoying beachgoers, but most of them were older men. No-one was ever charged with the murders.

When the Beaumont children disappeared from Glenelg just over 12 months later, it was tenuously linked in the press to the still-unsolved Wanda Beach murders in Sydney – the Christmas school holidays; children on a public beach; an unsolved crime.

In February 1966, the *Sydney Sun* newspaper sent a 'special investigator' to Adelaide to look into the Beaumont case. The *Adelaide Advertiser* wrote, 'One of Australia's most famous detectives, ex-Inspector Ray Kelly, who closed a colourful police career with the capture of Pentridge escapees Ryan and Walker in Sydney, is in Adelaide to try and find the three missing Beaumont children ... Mr Kelly made an unofficial visit to police headquarters yesterday to visit the Chief of the CIB (Superintendent Norm Lenton), who is a close friend, and other SA detectives who know him well.'

Ray 'Gunner' Kelly dined at an Adelaide restaurant with senior SAPOL detectives. A former member of South Australia's major crime squad recalled Kelly's visit. '"Gunner" Kelly was a good bloke,' he laughed. 'A big guy, six-foot-two and extremely well-dressed. He had Sydney by the short hairs, but it was a mistake for him to come over. But we all liked him. He was a real character.' Police stressed that he was there as a 'private citizen' and not on official police business.

Though popular with his South Australian colleagues, Kelly battled against inter-state rivalry between police departments. Kelly conducted his own door-knock along Brighton Road, investigating one woman's claim that she saw the man and the Beaumont children at about 2.45pm, and interviewing local postman Tom Patterson. Kelly then wished SAPOL 'all the success they richly deserve' and returned to Sydney the following day.

Over the years, both famous crimes – Wanda Beach and the Beaumonts – have remained unsolved, but having investigated and published accounts of both, I believe there is no real connection between the two. The Wanda Beach victims were teenage girls murdered in a frenzied sexual assault and the bodies were left at the crime scene. The Beaumonts were three children in another state, abducted from a public beach and never heard of again. They appear to be two quite separate crimes.

In 1973, however, the abduction of 11-year-old Joanne Ratcliffe and four-year-old toddler Kirste Gordon from the Adelaide Oval one Saturday afternoon offered many parallels with the mystery of the Beaumont children seven years before.

On Saturday 25 August 1973, Les Ratcliffe, a 38-year-old bread carter from the Adelaide suburb of Campbelltown, took his family to the Adelaide Oval to watch an Aussie Rules football match between Norwood and North Adelaide. Les, wife Kath, their 13-year-old son David and 11-year-old daughter Joanne sat in their usual spot in the Sir Edwin Smith Stand, surrounded by their friends and other Norwood supporters. By the time the first grade game started at about 1.30pm, a crowd of 12,000 people were watching the match.

Mrs Rita Huckel of Hackem was also at the Oval that day, with her four-year-old granddaughter Kirste Ann Gordon. Mrs Huckel's daughter and son-in-law, a schoolteacher at Adelaide Boys High, were away in Renmark over the weekend.

The Ratcliffes knew Mrs Huckel, but had not met Kirste before. When Kirste needed to go to the bathroom, Joanne offered to take her to the female toilets at the rear of the John Creswell Stand, on the other side of the Oval. In the third quarter of the main match, at about 3.45pm, Joanne again took Kirste to the toilet. When they didn't return after 10 or 15 minutes, Mr and Mrs Ratcliffe went looking for them.

When no trace of the girls could be found, Joanne's parents raced to the top of the Members Stand. Mrs Ratcliffe passed through a barricade and entered the Secretary's Office. The distraught mother asked that the Secretary of the SA Cricket Association, a Mr Munn, broadcast an appeal that two young girls were missing, but was told that the announcement could not be made during play because it would not be heard. She was told to return to her seat and see if the girls had come back and if they had not, to report the matter to a policeman. The parents reluctantly returned to their seats and the announcement wasn't made until five minutes after the end of play, at which point the girls were already gone.

That night, at about 9.00pm, the police contacted Mr and Mrs Gordon and informed them that their daughter was missing. The Gordons returned to Adelaide around midnight and Mr Gordon immediately went to the Adelaide Oval to join in the search. Les Ratcliffe accompanied detectives on a walk-through of his daughter's last known movements at the Adelaide Oval. Several times, Mr Ratcliffe broke down and cried in the arms of Detective Inspector Col Lehman, who was in charge of the case.

The missing children were described as follows:

Kirste Gordon: About 3 feet 4 inches tall, with blue eyes and of slim to medium build, with very fair English-type skin with faint freckles on either side of the nose. She has honey-blonde shoulder-length hair with a fringe and has a slight scar above the bridge of the nose. She has a birthmark on the base of the spine hairline. She was last seen wearing a white pleated skirt, purple jumper, and white panty hose with brown lace-up shoes.'

Joanne Ratcliffe: Motherly type, about 4 feet 2 inches tall, blue eyes, medium build, with dark brown hair worn in two pigtails tied with rubber bands. Last seen wearing a white blouse and white cardigan and mustard and black-banded tank top, black jeans, white track shoes and blue stripes, a white bra and coloured panties and white socks. Also wearing a marcasite watch and imitation gold chain and gold medallion in oval shape with a two-inch purple stone hanging about the middle of the chest.

Ken Wohling, the assistant curator of the Oval, said he'd seen a man with two girls at about 4.30pm, trying to entice some kittens from underneath a car that was parked in a large equipment shed, near the men's toilet behind the John Creswell Stand. Wohling later saw the man walking towards the southern gates, with the children following him. He was described as 5 feet 8 inches tall, wearing a brown hat with a wide brim, a grey-checked sports coat and brown trousers.

Wohling showed the detectives who had accompanied Les Ratcliffe to the Adelaide Oval where the man and girls had been. He told detectives that he was in the staffroom of the shed when he heard two girls calling, 'Puss, puss.' He then heard a man's voice say, 'I'll try and get him out for you.' Mr Wohling did not take much notice at the time, because there were many cats at the Adelaide Oval and children were always trying to play with them. 'I saw the man, from the back, walk towards the southern gate. He turned a bend and was gone.' The two girls followed the man a few yards behind. Wohling noticed that the man was stooped.

'Not long afterward, the father [of Joanne] came looking in the shed,' Wohling recalled. I said to him, 'They're not here!'

On the first day of the investigation, Superintendent Norm Lenton stated that the most important factor working against the police was time. 'We need help from the public now,' Lenton told the *Adelaide Advertiser*. 'It's no good someone ringing us with information in a week or even a few days … if anyone has any suspicions that someone may be an active sexual deviate, we want to know about it.' He then added chillingly, 'We don't want this to become another Beaumont case.'

Lenton added, 'From our knowledge of sexual deviates and their behavioural patterns, it seems most unlikely that this is the first time this man has molested young female children.' He implored anyone who might be shielding the abductor – perhaps because of blood ties, or out of a misplaced sense of loyalty – to come forward. 'Whoever is withholding information has a duty to help the police in the interests of these two missing girls or other children who may be in the same position in the future.'

Sheds and rubbish bins in every corner of the Adelaide Oval were searched, while other police groups searched the Festival Centre, the North Adelaide golf course and the railway yards. Police, on foot and in a boat, searched the Torrens River that runs through the Adelaide parklands; divers began at the northern bank of the City Bridge and searched 200 metres downstream. Roadblocks had quickly been set up and country-based police were already checking cars. Tip Top Bakery, which employed Les Ratcliffe, put all their vans on the road that Sunday so the drivers could look for any sign of the girls. It was like the search for the missing Beaumont children all over again.

On Tuesday night, 28 August, Les Ratcliffe appealed to his daughter's abductor on national television. 'Whoever is holding Joanne and Kirste, I am appealing to you personally to come forward or let them go,' he said. 'Drop them on some main street corner. I am sure my daughter will do the right thing and go straight to the nearest person she thinks she can trust. If you have any decency in you, any respect for these two children, who are only young children, 11 and four, who have never done any harm whatsoever ...

'If you've got them please look after them ... please, whatever you do, if you are sick or anything like that, I am sure if you come to the right authority they will help you ... if there is more than one of you, I would like the both of you to sit down and talk it over – I think you will find that talking will help a lot.'

When the South Australian Government posted only a modest $5,000 reward, 80 union workers employed by Babcock and Wilcox Australia Ltd on the Torrens Island power station donated a day's pay, which added a further $2,000 dollars to the award. Carpenters working on the city's Festival Hall building donated another $2,000. The Government later doubled its reward to $10,000 and offered a free pardon to any person who had knowledge of the crime but was not directly involved.

On 31 August, a 13-year-old boy who'd been selling sweets at the ground told the police he saw a man in a broad-brimmed hat dragging two girls outside the southern gate of the Adelaide Oval. A small girl who matched the description of Kirste Gordon was tucked under the man's right arm. The boy said that the man was also 'dragging a struggling, kicking girl', who fit the description of 11-year-old Joanne Ratcliffe. The older girl appeared to be trying to rescue the younger girl from the clutches of the man. The boy's description of a stooped, middle-aged man wearing a brown, broad-brimmed hat, grey check coat and brown trousers was identical to the man seen with the girls earlier.

The teenage witness said he had been standing under the archway underneath the Creswell Stand during the last quarter of the match when he saw the man 'swoop' on the girls from behind a pepper tree, taking Kirste under his right arm and then dragging Joanne alongside him as they walked towards the southern gateway. The older girl kicked and slapped the man as he grappled to hold the smaller girl under his arm and took them into the public car park.

'A picture is building up,' Senior Inspector Lehmann told the media, at a special press conference at Adelaide CIB. The man in question had been seen loitering at the ground since the morning of that Saturday. Did he befriend the girls – using the kittens near the equipment shed as a lure – when they left the adults in the grandstand? The police were able to track the man and the two girls for about '30 to 40 yards' into the public car park, but there was no further sign of them. They now appealed for anyone who was in the car park just before the end of the match to come forward.

An arts teacher at the SA School of Arts, Mr Waller, produced a watercolour impression of the main suspect based on Ken Wohling's description. The portrait appeared to match the published sketch of the man seen frolicking with the Beaumont children at Glenelg Beach in 1966, although the Adelaide Oval suspect was shorter and older, at 5 feet 8 inches, and the original veracity of the likeness of the man seen with the Beaumont children has always been in question.

A team of seven detectives, and 30 policemen and cadets, spent a week combing the street and knocking on the doors of approximately 1,000 homes in the local area. Despite cataloguing over 4,500 pieces of information, 400 letters of correspondence and another 400 enquiries from country areas and interstate, the investigation had not identified any known suspect by the time 1974 rolled around. This again left the door open for clairvoyants, charlatans and conmen to fill in the blanks.

In July 1974, journalist Dick Wordley travelled to Holland once more, to consult Gerard Croiset about the unsolved Beaumont case. He found the ageing clairvoyant gravely ill, having had half his stomach removed due to ulcers. When Wordley also mentioned the 'Adelaide Oval' case, Croiset said, 'You must see my son. My son will help you now.'

When Wordley spoke to Gerard Croiset Jnr, the young Dutchman quickly drew a sketch of the man, the house where the children were 'buried' and then made the startling prediction that the children's murderer would strike again 'somewhere in Australia during the current cycle of the moon'.

Wordley left Holland with the clairvoyant's visions of 'a farm, a red bus' and 'a high chimney'. Croiset Junior was later bought to Australia in July 1978 by the 0-10 television network. Detective Sergeant John McCall had a private meeting with Croiset before he left Australia. McCall had formed a very close relationship with Les Ratcliffe; he would regularly drop in on the Ratcliffe's modest housing estate home in Campbelltown and keep Les up to date with the investigation.

In December 1978, Les Ratcliffe called for a public inquest into the disappearance of the children and the subsequent police investigation. The main finding of the inquest, conducted by State Coroner Mr Ahern in July 1979, concerned the failure of the Secretary's Office at the Adelaide Oval to broadcast the parents' appeal about the missing children. For Les Ratcliffe, who desperately wanted the inquest to keep the case in the public eye, the open finding was not the end of the matter.

'I intend searching until I die or I catch the bastard, whichever comes first,' he said. Sadly it was to be the former. Suffering with cancer, the father of two dictated an open letter to the Adelaide public shortly before his death at age 46, in February 1981. 'Do not forget the Adelaide Oval abduction of August, 1973,' he wrote. 'As a parent I could not wish for anyone to live through what I have had to live through ... I do not want any sympathy. My family does not want sympathy ... the illness has caught me just when I was beginning to accept Joanne was gone forever ... despite it all, I am happy now.'

The Adelaide Oval abductions are regarded as the forgotten crime of this era, overshadowed by the Beaumont case. Was it possible that Adelaide produced two different child abductors, who both got away with the perfect crime? It seems unlikely. These two cases represented five children in seven years – the only recorded cases of multiple, unsolved abduction in Australia in the past 50 years.

* * *

During the years 1979 to 1983, the bodies of four young men were found in various parts of Adelaide, surgically mutilated or dismembered. Then, in June 1983, 15-year-old Richard Kelvin was abducted from a bus stop near his North Adelaide home. On 23 July, the boy's body was found in the Adelaide foothills. A post-mortem revealed that, although he had been missing for seven weeks, he had been kept alive for at least five weeks and his body contained traces of four different drugs.

The Adelaide media dubbed the killings 'The Family Murders' when detectives revealed the existence of an underground subculture of paedophilia and sexual sadism among the city's homosexual community, stretching back to the 1960s. One of the names in that network was Bevan Spencer von Einem, a tall, grey-haired, 37-year-old man. Von Einem denied any knowledge of the unsolved murders, but when police searched his house in Paradise, an Adelaide suburb, they discovered three of the drugs that had been found in Kelvin's body, and matched von Einem's hairs to those left on the boy's clothing. Of 525 fibres found on Richard Kelvin's body, 196 were found in von Einem's home or clothing. Five of von Einem's head hairs were found inside the boy's jeans and the dye that he used to mask his greying was found in those hairs.

Presented with forensic evidence that Kelvin had been in von Einem's home before he died, von Einem admitted that he met Kelvin on the day he disappeared. Von Einem stated that he was driving along O'Connell Street in North Adelaide on Sunday 5 June 1983, looking for a spot to park near some shops, when he almost hit Kelvin as the boy was jogging. The two began talking, von Einem said, and the conversation turned to problems Kelvin had been having at home and school. Kelvin willingly got into the car and they drove to von Einem's home. The 15-year-old stayed at von Einem's house for about two hours before he drove the boy into the Adelaide CBD and dropped him off beside a hospital, giving him $20 to catch a taxi home.

On 2 November 1984, von Einem was found guilty and sentenced to life imprisonment for the abduction and murder of Richard Kelvin. 'Life imprisonment' meant 25 years, with a non-parole period of 18 years, but this was doubled on appeal to a record 36 years non-parole period. While he was held in B Division of Yatala Labour Prison, detectives worked to build up a case to link him to other unsolved murders, but it would be six years before von Einem faced further charges.

At a committal hearing on 5 March 1990, an associate of von Einem, known only as 'Mr B', said that von Einem had killed at least 10 young people between 1966 and 1983, including the three Beaumont children, the two girls abducted from the Adelaide Oval, and the five murdered youths of 'The Family Murders' found between 1979 and 1983. During four days of testimony, Mr B described how he and von Einem would pick up hitchhikers, drug them and sexually abuse them. He said Von Einem would offer the young victims a combination of alcohol and the sedative Rohypnol, which rendered the victims unconscious and at the mercy of a number of paedophiles with whom von Einem operated. This happened about a dozen times, Mr B said. He had been with von Einem when he picked up Alan Barnes in June 1979, although he did not play any part in the murder of the teenager or the disposal of his body. Under cross-examination, Mr B said he was in fear of his life from another man who was with von Einem that night, and who was sitting in court that day. This man's identity was suppressed.

Distressingly, Mr B said that von Einem claimed to have performed some 'brilliant surgery' on the Beaumont children and that their bodies were buried in 'Moana or Myponga'. SAPOL would later conduct an extensive search of the Myponga Reservoir, but found nothing.

With these claims, many wondered if von Einem was the 'bogyman' Adelaide had been searching for all the years – or if that person still remained undetected.

Chapter 12

The Housekeeper

By the middle of 2007, a year after Stuart first spoke to Amanda, he had prepared a dossier of all the information he'd gathered about Hank Harrison and his family and sent it to SAPOL. When he didn't hear back, he phoned SAPOL and was told that his claims would be investigated. Stuart suggested that the family home where Hank's second wife now lived would be a good starting point, but a SAPOL detective said they had already spoken to Norma and had 'nothing further to go on'.

'I spoke to the detective about the £1 note given to Warwick and his friends,' Stuart later said, 'and I was told, "Oh well, they could have read about that in the book." I was beating my head up against a brick wall. The original police investigation viewed the 'pound note' given to the Beaumont children to buy their lunch as an integral part of the case – it was very unusual for the time – and yet now, it didn't raise any eyebrows. They just brushed it off.'

The jigsaw puzzle of evidence was coming together, however, and Stuart was being drawn inexorably into the middle of it. 'The facts were the facts,' Stuart said. 'I wasn't making up these allegations ... other people were saying these things. All I wanted was for SAPOL to check them out, or I was going to check them out myself.'

After several months of what felt like stonewalling from a

SAPOL detective, Stuart decided to talk to Norma himself. He was able to get Brian McHenry, the former financial controller of Hank's company, to introduce him. Although Stuart had already revealed to McHenry the real reasons he was looking into Hank's background, McHenry called Norma and suggested that she meet 'a guy researching Hank's background and his business'.

'Brian had an opportunity to tell Norma the real reason why I wanted to speak to her, but he didn't, as he felt it was best for me to discuss the issues face to face with her,' Stuart explained. 'Perhaps he also wanted to find out more about his old boss; he'd been very helpful and understanding.'

Stuart wrote to Norma initially, but it was only after Brian contacted her personally that she agreed to meet him. Standing outside the Harrison family home in the heart of Glenelg, Stuart was uncharacteristically nervous, given what he now knew. I was lecturing at university at the time, and Stuart rang me before going inside. 'If I don't ring you in a couple of hours,' he said, 'you ring me. It will give me an excuse to leave.'

I thought Stuart was being a little melodramatic, but agreed it was important someone else knew where he was and what he was doing. We laughed about it at the time, but later he remarked, quite seriously, 'This is a case that has been unsolved for many years and it's been unsolved for a reason. Somebody has been able to cover their tracks all these years.'

I was concerned Stuart was getting too close to the case, but as it happened, this encounter with Norma would be a major turning point in his investigation.

Stuart was greeted warmly by Norma, a small woman in her early sixties. After offering his business card and exchanging pleasantries, they sat down at the kitchen table. Norma walked Stuart through several folders of family photographs. There were only a handful of

Hank – one on the beach with three friends, smiling into the sun; another of a tennis match with some of the same friends, about ten years later. There was one of Hank in a suit, and Anya wearing a black dress, but none of Hank and Warwick. One of the older photos was of a little girl sitting on a tricycle in a flowery white dress, Hank's niece perhaps; Norma didn't know who it was. The last was of Hank, aged five, wearing a silk dress.

Stuart told Norma straight away that he'd come to talk about Hank's relationship with his son Warwick. 'Oh God, what's he up to?' she said, throwing her hands in the air. Stuart told her that Warwick had made some allegations regarding Hank, claiming that he'd been sexually abused by his father and that Hank had something to do with the disappearance of the three Beaumont children from Glenelg Beach. When Stuart showed her a copy of my 2006 book about the case, Norma snatched the photos off the table and left the book there without touching it.

Stuart could see she was immediately annoyed. She became fidgety. 'The Beaumont children?' Norma asked. 'That's the same as Joanne Ratcliffe and Kirste Gordon at the Adelaide Oval.'

Stuart thought this was a strangely automatic association. 'You certainly know your history,' he said.

Stuart reassured Norma that he wasn't suggesting Hank had anything to do with the disappearance of the children; he was only following up Warwick's allegations. 'I said to her that I knew an officer at SAPOL had visited her to discuss these issues and she said, "I haven't had any discussion with SAPOL." … That really spurred me on to find the truth.

'I said to Norma that what Warwick was alleging about Hank could be completely wrong. She went into a long diatribe about Warwick – that he was an alcoholic, all he does is call and ask for money and leave silly messages on her voicemail. She played me one of the messages he had left her and he was obviously drunk. "This is what I have to put up with," she said.'

'I felt for her,' Stuart admitted, 'and I was trying to put her at ease, but I needed to find out if what Warwick had said was true or not.'

Stuart bought up the issue of the safe in the cellar. Amanda had said this was where Hank kept his guns. 'Did Warwick tell you that?' Norma asked. When Stuart said it was Amanda, Norma snapped, 'That Amanda, all she's after is money.'

Norma said the only safe in the house was upstairs in the main bedroom, and offered to show Stuart around the house. 'Norma was quite happy to show me through every room,' Stuart recounted. There was a large attic and a cellar, just as Amanda had described. The cellar was a very cool place; there was one small window, a cement floor and shelving on which old vases and books had been carefully placed. The books were in pristine condition, which Stuart put down to the cool climate and the lack of sunlight and dust. There were all kinds of objects down there, including an old printing press. Stuart commented that it would be worth a lot of money in an op shop, and Norma shook her head and agreed. 'There was also a stack of old brown, vinyl briefcases, like ones your grandfather might have had,' Stuart told me. 'I could not believe the condition they were in. It was if they were brand new.'

Sitting on top of one of the briefcases was a small purse, whitish in colour, with silver trim at the top and two baubles that wrapped around one another and clicked the purse closed. 'It was a type of small purse that many little girls would have had in the 1950s and 1960s,' Stuart said. 'I thought it was very odd that a little girl's purse was just sitting there like that. Again, it was in pristine condition. Hank had a son and grandson, so the girl's purse just stuck out among the items there. I didn't say anything at the time, but I remembered Jane Beaumont was carrying a purse with her when she went missing. It was very odd, sitting there.'

Norma took Stuart upstairs and said she'd show him where the family safe was. Stuart said he didn't need to see it, but Norma insisted. 'We sat in the lounge room talking for another half an hour after that. I didn't want to talk about Warwick's abuse too much. I asked Norma if she had contacted Amanda to say she'd heard Warwick was abused by his father. Norma dismissed it all out of hand.'

When Stuart came out of the house, he rang me straight away. 'Did one of the Beaumont girls have a purse?' he asked me.

'Jane Beaumont carried the money her mother gave her in a small white purse,' I said.

Stuart told me he'd seen a girl's purse in the cellar, and gave a brief description of it. I said he had to go back and get it. Make any excuse, I told him – beg, borrow or steal it if you have to. It could be crucial.

Stuart couldn't just march back inside; it would look too suspicious. He would go back the next day, he said. He hadn't asked Norma anything about the purse, so it should be still sitting there if he went back inside. He bought a bunch of flowers and sent them around to Norma with a message, saying he was sorry to have imposed upon her, that it was lovely to meet her, and thanking her for her time. Stuart called Norma later that evening and said there was something else he needed to discuss. Could he come around and see her again tomorrow?

When Stuart called in the following morning, Norma had another woman with her. The atmosphere was decidedly cold, so Stuart got straight to the point. 'It's regarding the girl's purse I saw down in the cellar,' he told her. 'Could I have another look at it?' When the group went downstairs, the purse was still there, and Stuart made the mistake of saying Jane Beaumont had a white purse with her the day she disappeared.

'I was trying not to spook her, but Norma immediately became defensive and her back stiffened,' Stuart recalled. '"No, no, no. I bought that at an op shop last week," she stammered. These were the same words I'd used the day before, when we were talking about the printing press – "the op shop". She opened the purse and I could see that inside it was a silky material, fawn in colour.'

Why would Norma, who had recently inherited millions of dollars, buy a child's purse in an op shop? For whom? And why was it downstairs in the cellar?

Norma then told Stuart that she'd like him to leave. 'Yes, thank you,' her friend nodded. The mood had changed again.

'They didn't want me there, so I left,' Stuart said. 'Maybe I was too personal, but it raised a lot of questions for me. I don't think Norma knew the purse was there or had ever noticed it, but once I mentioned Jane Beaumont had a white purse, the walls went up.'

Stuart contacted SAPOL once again and informed them of the discovery of the girl's purse. Days later, a detective went to visit Norma, but the former housekeeper told the detective she had thrown the purse out. SAPOL still didn't seem to think that Norma's behaviour was suspicious, or if they did, they didn't let on to Stuart. A detective tried to placate him, saying, 'Mate, you're chasing your tail.' Stuart replied, 'And if the tail gets long enough, I'm going to catch it.'

'I couldn't believe it,' Stuart said. 'Why would she throw the purse out, unless it was something to hide? It was just very suspicious.'

A week later, Stuart received a long legal letter from Hank's lawyers, acting on behalf of Norma. It stated that he had been an unwanted presence in the house (even though he had been invited), that he was making unfounded accusations about her late husband, and most importantly, that he'd misrepresented himself as a local historian (which he was – of sorts). 'I wrote a very detailed and a very respectful return letter, covering every single point,' Stuart remembered. 'If I was an unwanted presence in that house, then how was I allowed to stay there for two hours? And why did she say yes when I asked if I could come back the following day?' After sending his letter in response, Stuart heard nothing more about it.

Norma had been a housekeeper from a modest background. She inherited more than a million dollars in Hank's will, plus the house. Was she frightened of losing the money? Did she think Warwick would make some claim on the estate if it was proven his father had abused him? Was she trying to protect her husband's reputation? Whatever her reasoning, Stuart understood her fear.

'It would be hard for people to accept that somebody they knew was a paedophile,' Stuart reasoned. 'I wouldn't want to talk to someone who was trying to tell me that either, so I don't blame her at all.' He later found out that Norma had contacted Hank's former colleagues and peripheral family members and told them not to talk to him. But it didn't matter. It only made Stuart want to dig deeper.

Months later, Stuart had a phone call from one of his contacts in Adelaide. The Harrison family house was on the market. The home, which had been in the family for almost a century, had been cleaned out and now stood empty. Stuart immediately went to Adelaide and found that the house was indeed vacant. On a hunch that Norma might have sold off items to the local second-hand shops, if she hadn't just dumped the lot in the bin, he visited a couple of op shops in the area, but couldn't find the white purse.

The universe plays interesting tricks on us, though. As the writer Norman Mailer once observed, 'the cosmos likes to strew coincidences around the rim of a funnel, around which huge events are converging', to keep you on track or throw you off-kilter. While looking for the white purse in a Salvation Army shop, Stuart instead happened upon a 1960 paperback edition of *Little Women*.

It had a price sticker on it, $1.99, but that had been recently added. Stuart saw that the paperback was almost 50 years old, but looked as if it hadn't been read in a long time. Not a page was out of place.

Stuart had visited the shop three weeks earlier and had not seen the paperback then. Who had brought it in?

Stuart gently picked up the book and opened the inside cover, to see if the name 'Jane Beaumont', or 'JB' perhaps, was written inside in a child's hand. It wasn't, but he was not going to be caught out again. He purchased the book and has it in his keeping.

'Every time I was in Adelaide after that (and I used to be there every two or three months during this period) I would go to that op shop just in case something else turned up,' Stuart admitted. He didn't turn up anything else, but still hopes for a 'long shot' – that somebody might have heard about someone investigating the unsolved case, panicked, and given incriminating items to a charity shop, such as Arnna's headband, Grant's sandal or the children's carry bag.

Often, Stuart found himself at the factory Hank had owned in Adelaide, walking the perimeter and scanning the vast concrete surface for any evidence of a sandpit that might have existed in the 1960s. He found none – just hectares of concrete.

'It's ironic,' Stuart said to me one day, when we were discussing the case.

'What's that?' I asked.

'Croiset, the clairvoyant.'

'What about him?'

'He said the children's bodies were buried in a pit under a concrete floor.'

* * *

It had been 12 months since Amanda first contacted us, and

Stuart had done a great job 'reconstructing' the life of Hank Harrison, chipping away at his public profile and his private persona. He had verified everything Amanda had told us — that Warwick claimed to have been sexually abused by his father, and said he saw the Beaumont children in the backyard the day they disappeared; that Hank had a 'satin fetish' and found it difficult to control himself; that he matched the physical description of the man seen playing with the children at Colley Reserve; that he had a habit of giving £1 notes to children to get them to do what he wanted; that he lived within walking distance of the cake shop where the children were last seen; and that Hank had the run of a factory with a large 'sandpit'.

Stuart talked openly and often about the unsolved case, and myself and several other friends were starting to get concerned. 'Do us one favour,' a friend said over beers at a family barbecue, as Stuart reeled off another long story about the Beaumont investigation. 'Just don't get obsessed by this.'

It was clear that Stuart felt a special connection with the case. He had been the same age as Arnna (born 1958) and lived in the local area when the tragedy happened. Over the past ten years, he has said to me many times, 'I'd just like the parents to know what happened to their kids. I want to know the truth.'

'Remember what happened to the newsreader Brian Taylor,' I reminded him, not to mention Stan Swaine and Con Polites. They all became deeply involved in the case, and suffered great disappointment over the false trails laid down by clairvoyants and charlatans.

'That's not me,' Stuart assured me. He was very wary of the case taking over his life. With a young family and a successful business to run, he was confident he had it all under control.

'I don't want to solve it,' Stuart confided once. 'I just want SAPOL to act on what we know and tell us we are wrong ... that Warwick

Harrison is wrong and that Hank had nothing to do with this.'

After 12 months of hard work, and hundreds of hours of investigation at his own expense, Stuart had nowhere to go. He didn't want to deal with SAPOL anymore, and he was sure they'd had enough of him too, so he did something very sensible. He decided to walk away from the Beaumont case and give everything he had compiled to a private investigator.

Stuart asked Mostyn 'Moss' Matters – the detective at Glenelg police station on the day the three Beaumont children were reported missing – to recommend the best investigator in Adelaide, someone who could look into this new information and tell him where he was wrong.

Moss recommended Bill Hayes.

Chapter 13

Other Voices

There have been many theories about what happened to the Beaumont children over the years, each investigated by police and ultimately rejected. Several potential suspects have been brought to light in the public arena, but no charges have been laid. SAPOL says they receive half-a-dozen 'breakthroughs' a month, but the Beaumont case remains open to this day.

In 1970, SAPOL had imported and installed a 'unique card index detection system' developed by Scotland Yard, which allowed for the 'comprehensive cataloguing of information' supplied by the public and, more importantly, prioritised the information as it came in. The system was installed by UK detectives in response to an ongoing investigation, known as 'the Duncan Case'. On the night of 10 May 1972, Dr George Duncan, a gay university lecturer, was bashed by several men and thrown into the Torrens River, where he drowned. A second man was also thrown into the water that night (this was not revealed to the media at the time). He saw Dr Duncan struggling in the water, but could not help him because he was injured. The second man was helped to shore by a 26-year-old accountant named Bevan Spencer von Einem – the now-convicted child predator who, by astounding coincidence, was also on the banks of the Torrens that night and took the man to hospital.

Before the new system was put in place, police had not been able to identify the man's attackers, but the new case management system organised thousands of bits of information from the public about the nocturnal world of casual gay relationships on the banks of the Torrens, and the 'poofter bashings' that plagued the area. The new system uncovered a startling piece of information – it was alleged that a group of vice squad detectives had regularly assaulted, then thrown into the river, homosexual men who were 'cottaging' for partners. After a lengthy investigation, two former detectives were charged with the manslaughter of Dr Duncan in the early 1980s, but were found not guilty. The system also introduced Bevan von Einem to SAPOL, though his involvement in the 'Duncan case' appeared to be purely circumstantial.

In 1973, with the abduction of Joanne and Kirste from the Adelaide Oval, the new system swung into action. Under the old police 'running sheet' procedure, calls would be typed up and added to an ever-growing stack of paper, but now information was indexed and prioritised with an allocated action. 'Priority one' calls demanded immediate action, 'priority two' meant that work needed to be done, but not urgently, and 'priority three' was allocated to calls that did not require an action, with the card being filed for future reference. This new system used cadets, administrative staff and junior officers to type the cards, then called in investigators to prioritise and cross-reference information.

The strength of the new system was that more than one officer could prioritise calls; previously, any investigating officer could write 'AAC' (All Appeared Correct) at the top of a report and that would be the end of the matter. With new possibilities for cross-referencing, vital leads turned up, which could then be allocated a suitable amount of police resources and effectively investigated.

In the late 1970s and early 1980s, the bodies of five young men were found dumped in various parts of Adelaide. The victims had been surgically mutilated or dismembered, and most had numerous prescription drugs in their systems when they were killed. 'The Family Murders', as they became known, were named after an alleged network of sadistic paedophiles operating in Adelaide – a group including lawyers, judges, police, doctors and assorted businessmen – who apparently fed into each other and protected one another from detection.

Bevan Spencer von Einem, the 'hero' of the Duncan case, became linked to the Family Murders through his contact with known paedophiles, and because his name was on a prescription drug database. Teenager Richard Kelvin, the last of the five victims, had some of these drugs in his system when he was murdered, and police later discovered forensic links to von Einem's house on the victim's body.

After being sentenced for Kelvin's murder, von Einem's associate, 'Mr B', linked him to the Family Murders, and the Beaumont and Adelaide Oval abductions. But in lifting suppression orders against the publication of these allegations, Magistrate David Gurry was scathing about 'the piecemeal and selective nature' of Mr B's disclosures to the police and the court. The allegations were impossible to prove. Where were the bodies?

In June of 1990, lawyers acting for Bevan von Einem filed an application seeking the 'quashing, dismissing or permanent staying of the charges, on the ground that the proceedings were an abuse of process … the application was based mainly on the assertion that von Einem could not be guaranteed a fair trial, as a result of the media publicity of a prejudicial nature'. In December 1990, the Attorney General advised the Crown prosecution to enter a motion of *nolle prosequi* – the charge against von Einem relating to Mark Langley, one of the victims among The Family Murders, would not proceed due to lack of evidence.

In 2007, Channel 7 invited me to look at archival footage of the draining of Patawalonga Boat Haven in 1966, following the disappearance of the Beaumont children. An enterprising researcher had spotted what he thought was a young Bevan von Einem standing on a pier. It was interesting from an historical point of view – people who have committed murders often join in on the search for victims, so they can relive their crime – but then, most of the population of Adelaide watched the search for the children. It looked as though it could have been von Einem – there is a widely published image of him from the Duncan case, as a 26-year-old in 1972 – but six years earlier, he seemed to have a student's beard and his hair was fair.

Although von Einem was the right height and build as the man seen with the Beaumont children, he was only 19 years old when the children disappeared in 1966. That didn't match the description of the Beaumont case suspect, who was in his 'late 30s or early 40s'. Interestingly, when the Adelaide Oval abductions occurred in 1973, Bevan von Einem was living with his mother in the Adelaide suburb of Campbelltown – the same suburb as the home of one of the victims, Joanne Ratcliffe. Was it another macabre co-incidence? He looked nothing like the suspect in that crime, but could he have been involved?

A former SAPOL detective told me that they knew Bevan von Einem was at Glenelg the day 'The Pat' was drained, because they interviewed him in the 1980s, after Mr B's sensational allegations were first published. Von Einem, however, denied any knowledge about the five missing children.

If he was responsible for the five young men grouped together in the Family Murders, then Bevan von Einem was no master criminal. The bodies of all five victims – Alan Barnes and Neil Muir (1979), Peter Stogneff (1981), Mark Langley and Richard Kelvin (1983) –

were found dumped in locations around Adelaide. If von Einem was involved in the Beaumont and the Adelaide Oval cases, why didn't he hide the bodies of these five victims in the same place he hid the still-undiscovered children? And as he was in jail without the chance of parole, wouldn't the now-66-year-old give up his accomplices? There might be honour among thieves, but not among paedophiles who prey on defenceless children. There is a record $1 million reward for information leading to the conviction of those responsible for the Family Murders.

In 2004, Victorian Police confirmed they had launched a fresh inquiry into paedophile Derek Ernest Percy, who'd been jailed for the murder of a young girl in 1969. Percy, at the time a 21-year-old naval cadet stationed at *HMAS Cerberus* in Melbourne, was charged with the mutilation and murder of 12-year-old Yvonne Tuohy at the Westernport Bay fishing village at Warneet, but was found not guilty by reason of insanity. Percy was 'confined to safe custody at the Governor's pleasure', nominally for a period of 25 years, but has remained in jail, still classed a threat to society.

In February 2005, Victorian, New South Wales, South Australian and Federal Police questioned Percy about the disappearance of the three Beaumont children and several other unsolved crimes, including the 1965 rapes and murders of Christine Sharrock and Marianne Schmidt at Wanda Beach, the strangulation murder of six-year-old Canberra schoolboy Allen Redston on 27 September 1966, the murder of four-year-old Simon Brook on 18 May 1968 in the inner Sydney suburb of Glebe, and the disappearance of seven-year-old Linda Stilwell from the Melbourne beachside suburb of St Kilda on 10 August 1968.

Percy is known to have been in NSW in 1965 (Wanda) and 1968 (Brook), and was in Melbourne in 1968 (Stillwell) and 1969 (Tuohy). Since 2006, Percy has faced coronial inquests for the unsolved murders of Simon Brook and Linda Stillwell, but has not been committed to trial due to a lack of evidence and the now-65-year-old's mental state. Having written a book on Percy (*Derek Percy: Australian Psycho*, 2008) and interviewed both AFP and SAPOL detectives, I believe Percy did not have anything to do with the murder of Allen Redston, or the disappearance of the Beaumont children. In September 1966, when Allen's body was found gagged and hog-tied in a local creek, Derek Percy was a high-school student, 400 kilometres away at Mount Beauty in north-western Victoria. The AFP believe that Redston's death may have been the result of a bullying incident gone wrong, and the person responsible was a local boy who was interviewed in the original investigation, but not charged due to lack of evidence.

It has been suggested that Derek Percy was on holiday with his parents in Adelaide in January 1966, but this was denied by a family member, whom I interviewed for my 2008 book. Other writers have promoted the theory that Percy was at Glenelg on Australia Day 1966, but he was barely 17 years old and does not match the physical description of the man seen playing with the Beaumont children at Colley Reserve anyway. Even if Percy was there, where would a 17-year-old hide the bodies of three small children when he is on holidays with his parents, cannot drive a car and doesn't know the lay of the land?

In 2005, claims by the Tasmanian Commissioner of Police, Richard McCreadie, that convicted child killer James O'Neill 'could be responsible' for the abduction of the three Beaumont children were quickly dismissed by SAPOL. McCreadie was the arresting officer in 1975, when O'Neill was charged with the murder of nine-year-old Ricky John Smith and sentenced to life imprisonment. O'Neill, who had travelled extensively throughout Australia – including the opal fields of South Australia – later confessed to another murder.

O'Neill was also investigated over the abduction and sexual assault of four boys in Victoria in the early 1970s.

Detective Superintendent Peter Woite told the media that James O'Neill had been recently interviewed by SAPOL and 'discounted from our inquiries'. It appeared O'Neill's only link to the Beaumont children was that he may have driven through Adelaide on his way to the opal fields in January 1966 – hardly enough to call O'Neill a 'person of interest'.

When I met *The Age* journalist Andrew Rule in 2006, he told me to have a close look at Queenslander Arthur Stanley Brown, the main suspect in the double murder of young sisters Judith and Susan Mackay in Townsville on 26 August 1970. It was thought that Brown, who looked uncannily like the sketch of the Adelaide Oval suspect, right down to the broad-brimmed hat he wore on his travels interstate, might have been in Adelaide working at the Festival Hall building site at the time. If Brown had abducted Joanne Ratcliffe and Kirste Gordon, snatching them in an opportunistic raid before he headed home to Townsville, he would have driven via the Flinders Highway and could have disposed of the bodies anywhere.

Arthur Brown was 61 years old in 1973, and the same height as the suspect, but would not have matched the athletic, 6 foot tall Beaumont suspect (Brown was aged 53 in January 1966, but was fit and wiry). When Brown's photo was published around the country, his long, gaunt face eerily matched the sketches of the Beaumont and the Adelaide Oval suspects. Major Crime Superintendent Paul Schramm was forced to comment on the growing media speculation about Brown's possible involvement in the unsolved Adelaide crimes. 'I agree there is some similarity,' Schramm told John Merriman in the *Advertiser*, 'but I would stress that at this stage that is purely coincidental and in itself doesn't amount to any evidence that Mr Brown has had anything to do with the matters in SA.'

A former Adelaide woman living in Victoria saw Brown's photo in the newspaper, alongside the suspect's sketch. Although she had not come forward in 1973 when Joanne and Kirste were abducted, the woman told the media she believed it was Arthur Brown she saw struggling with two young girls, as she walked with her family from Adelaide Zoo all those years ago. SAPOL, however, could not rely on the woman's identification, because the suspect's photo had been published in the media and the woman had not selected Brown from a photo 'line-up'.

In 1998, 86-year-old Arthur Brown was finally charged with the rape and murder of Judith and Susan Mackay in Townsville in 1970. Brown was a 58-year-old maintenance man with the Queensland Public Works Department when the bodies of the sisters, aged five and seven, were found in a dry creek bed. Brown pleaded not guilty to the charges, and was later released, when the jury in his 1999 trial could not reach a verdict, and authorities declined to proceed with another trial because of Brown's age and alleged dementia. Arthur Brown was officially eliminated as a suspect in the Beaumont and the Adelaide Oval cases in 2001. He passed away in 2004 without facing any of the 45 charges – including murder, rape, sodomy, deprivation of liberty and administering drugs – that had been brought against him.

With the main 'persons of interest' linked to the Beaumont case over the past 30 years – Bevan von Einem, Derek Percy, Arthur Brown and James O'Neill – having been thoroughly investigated, and no charges laid, we hoped SAPOL would welcome a new 'person of interest' to look into. We had found a man who matched the description of the Beaumont suspect, lived 500 metres from where the children disappeared, was alleged to be a paedophile by his own family members, and could have used his wealth and position to get away with murder.

* * *

In late 2011, Stuart read a news article concerning sexual abuse allegations made by Thomas Hendricks, a respected Adelaide community leader. Hendricks claimed to have been sexually abused over a 10-year period in the late 1950s and early 1960s by members of the clergy – allegations that are being seriously and vigorously investigated at the present time. At the time of the disappearance of the Beaumont children, Thomas lived and worked in Glenelg, where most of the abuse was alleged to have taken place. Stuart decided to contact him to see if might know anything about Hank Harrison. Stuart stated in his email to Hendricks that he too had grown up in the Glenelg area during the 1960s, and was researching prominent Glenelg individuals – businessman, sportspeople and clergy. In a second email, he asked if Thomas had ever met Hank Harrison.

Stuart received no reply. He had made no mention of the Beaumont case or the specifics of the research he was doing at the time, so he was surprised by Hendricks' lack of response. After a week or two, he decided to phone Thomas directly, having tracked down the number online. When Thomas Hendricks picked up the phone, Stuart introduced himself. Stuart found him to be quietly spoken, and intelligent and measured in his use of words, and they enjoyed a long chat about Glenelg and its history.

When Thomas confirmed he had once lived in the heart of Glenelg, close to the Harrison family home, Stuart asked him if he had ever heard of or met Hank Harrison. Thomas hesitated for quite some time, before replying, 'Yes.' Stuart could hear the concern in his voice. Thomas added slowly, 'In certain circles.' When Stuart asked what Thomas meant about 'certain circles' the elderly academic replied, 'Well, in the 1960s and 1970s they didn't have the name we give them today, but they were "paedophilic circles".'

Thomas said Hank's name had 'popped up' several times when abuse occurred at the hands of another paedophile, whom he named. He went on to say that in his early teens, when he was at the mercy of his abusers, he sat in the back of a car that was being driven by a senior member of the clergy and a well-dressed businessman. The adults would stop outside private boys' schools to 'admire' the students. Thomas claimed that, at the time, this sort of behaviour was 'acceptable' among a small, select group – a group with power, wealth and influence, which Thomas had experienced firsthand.

Stuart informed Thomas of the true nature of his research. Thomas knew the Beaumont story well, and agreed to meet with us in Adelaide. 'You didn't really know who I was, yet you gave out personal information,' Stuart commented. Thomas' reply spoke to the nature of the man on the other end of the line: 'Stuart, I have nothing to hide.'

We sat down with Thomas Hendricks in his Adelaide home in February 2012. We spoke for almost two hours, discussing everything from the history of the state to religious suppression and sexual misconduct across the various social classes.

Up until the early 1970s, homosexuality was a criminal act in all Australian states, so some homosexuals married or joined the Church. 'The Church is a very conducive place for homosexuality,' Thomas said. He claimed there were religious groups who had been openly homosexual and clearly identified themselves as gay, and that various homosexual and heterosexual circles had overlapped with paedophile circles – especially in Adelaide.

Thomas said that many people had not forgiven former Premier Don Dunston for making Adelaide's 'dark side part of its public life' in the 1970s: 'Homosexuality was decriminalised; Maslins Beach became Australia's first nude beach; pornography was viewed as art and *Playboy* magazine was sold in corner shops, not just at the airport; then the Duncan Case challenged the nature of policy and hastened the decriminalisation of homosexuality.'

According to Thomas, 'The Family' was a very real presence in Adelaide until the crimes of Bevan von Einem flushed their activities into the open in 1980s. 'The Family' had strong connections in North Adelaide, allegedly a centre of paedophilia. A group will protect itself, Thomas pointed out, whether it's a business, the Church or a criminal group, so it was difficult for someone like him, who had suffered abuse, to find justice; his abusers were very-well protected.

When we asked Thomas about Hank Harrison, he said that he knew Harrison was an associate of a known paedophile, whose name was later verified for us by SAPOL.

We wished Thomas well in his fight for justice; meanwhile, he had provided us with enough information to suggest we were on the right track, and that Harrison's connections could have protected him for all those years.

Chapter 14

Brothers in Arms

Mostyn 'Moss' Matters was the detective at Glenelg police station the day the Beaumont children were reported missing. Stuart Mullins met and interviewed the retired detective in 2007, not realising until much later that Mostyn was in fact a cousin of his, Stuart's, mother. They met regularly over the next five years, and Stuart struck up an easy rapport with the retired detective, who was quiet and reserved, but a natural story-teller.

'In the early 1960s I had aspirations of being a detective,' Moss recalled. 'As a stepping stone to the CIB, quite a few of the traffic officers where I was stationed went into the Vice Squad and from there into the CIB. The Vice Squad investigated licensing offences, gaming issues and prostitution, and I was sent down to one of the hotels in Port Adelaide to gather evidence against the local bookmaker.' At the time, Mostyn wasn't a drinker, so he stood up at the bar drinking lemon squash all afternoon, waiting for the bookmaker to show. By the time five o'clock arrived, the publican came up to him and said, 'Look, son, if you want to catch the bookie, you'll have to drink something stronger than squash.'

The next week, he was sent to another hotel at Port Adelaide with the same assignment. This time, he ordered a schooner of beer at the bar. One schooner led to another, then another, and by the time five o'clock came round, the young detective was 'legless' and the publican had to ring the police to come and collect him. Needless to say, no bookie was caught that day either.

But Mostyn Matters learned quickly, and became a respected detective at Glenelg. Former and serving detectives Stuart spoke to over the years described Mostyn as a very dedicated, 'no bullshit' officer, who got the job done and done well.

'The Glenelg Branch had a number of quality constables and detectives,' Moss told us. 'Pieter Vogel, Lloyd Brand, Nick Drymalik and Detective Sergeant Ron Blight, Head of the Glenelg CIB.' He loved his work and was proud of his career with SAPOL.

We were interested in Mostyn's memories of the Beaumont case, hoping to gain an understanding of what it must have been like that Australia Day when a 'visibly upset' Grant and Nancy Beaumont came into the station to report their children missing. We were also interested in how the investigation unfolded, and Mostyn's thoughts on the information that had been forwarded to us by members of the Harrison family.

What stood out most for him, Stuart asked, when he looked back at the initial investigation? 'The absolute utter frustration of no one coming forward,' Mostyn said. 'We had bugger all to go on and a lack of manpower to do the job.' The investigating team held up as best they could – they had a job to do – but battled against an overwhelming amount of contradictory information, with only a small staff.

'In those days we had only one telephone line at Glenelg to take the calls,' Mostyn recalled. 'Plus, we had to take individual statements by hand and then type them up. It was an impossible task.'

What the public did not see, Mostyn said, was the painstaking behind-the-scenes work that went on during the investigation. 'The person-to-person contact with the public,' Mostyn said, 'and standing alongside the Beaumonts ... advising, caring, counselling and consoling. Seeing and feeling the devastating effects these events had on the parents and close family members – it took its toll on everyone, especially the policemen involved. It profoundly affected everyone.'

Mostyn and his colleague, Detective Sergeant Blight, spent many days with Mr and Mrs Beaumont during the initial investigation and in the years that followed. Moss still talks to Grant Beaumont, even though he has long since retired from SAPOL.

'"Wings" Blight was already a heavy smoker and he was the type of dedicated detective that took issues home with him,' Mostyn remembered. Blight was said to be a natural worrier at the best of times, and Mostyn suspected this eventually led to his death in the late 1990s, but there was no doubt he loved his job. 'Ron was one of the best police investigators in Adelaide – he could relate to the worst criminals and, with an excellent command of the English language, could pry the best information from the most hardened of suspects. His questioning techniques were far superior to anyone in the force.'

Mostyn remembered that Australia Day in 1966 as being 'very hot, very humid ... a scorcher ... and the parks around the Glenelg beachfront were packed with people. To even notice three children among the thousands of children there that day was impossible,' he said. 'They would have melted into the crowd ... '

When the children were reported missing, Mostyn said, it was thought they had caught the wrong bus home or gone to a friend's place, but as time wore on, the concern for their safety started to grow. 'And once it was reported in the media that three children were missing, the switchboard at Glenelg police station ran hot,' he recalled. 'The main switchboard was located in the front section of the police station. The CIB office was located in the witness room at the local court adjoining the station. It was so small you couldn't swing a cat in it.'

Calls were received from concerned, well-meaning members of the public and people arrived in person at the Glenelg police station. Police also had to deal with the media – radio, TV and newspapermen – all trying to do their job and unearth some new angle on the story. During the initial hours, the team also had to keep a distraught Mr and Mrs Beaumont calm, as well as remaining professional and aloof about what was unfolding.

'It was hard,' Mostyn admitted. 'Many of us had children of our own. This had never happened before – three members of a family, missing from a public place, possibly abducted, and the whole thing was puzzling from the start.' And the workload didn't get any easier. 'Fifteen to sixteen hours a day, seven days a week, was the norm, month after month,' recalled Mostyn. 'There was no paid overtime in those days and your family life suffered. The media was all over the shop and we still had our normal enquiries coming in. In the scheme of things, however, this was "small stuff" compared to what had happened, what the parents were going through.'

From his perspective, Mostyn's main criticism of the investigation was a lack of assistance from head office. Several other former detectives we spoke to in the course of writing this book supported his claim. 'There was little or no assistance from Adelaide CIB,' one said. The request went out from Glenelg CIB to Adelaide CIB when the investigation was at its most crucial stage, but the detectives we spoke to alleged that no more detectives were sent over to work on the case. Senior officers later went over Superintendent Lenton's head, we were told, going straight to the police commissioner to request extra men.

Moss had expected the talented and respected Ron Blight to continue leading the investigation, but after 12 months, Stan 'Tonner' Swaine was made head of Adelaide CIB. In Mostyn's opinion – one shared by other former detectives we spoke to – Swaine was easily distracted by new leads. 'Stan kept to himself,' Mostyn claimed. 'He did not liaise with the rest of the team and was hardly at the station … he was off following one red herring or another.'

Glenelg CIB wanted nothing to do with the clairvoyant Gerard Croiset, brought to Adelaide by Col Polites and Brian Blackwell in November 1966. 'There is no disrespect to Mr Blackwell or Mr Polites,' Mostyn said. 'They had their hearts in the right place and spent their own money to have the warehouse floor in Paringa Park dug up. At least they tried.'

Mostyn Matters moved on from Glenelg CIB in 1971, but continued to answer many enquires about the Beaumont case over the years. He met people with information regarding the unsolved case, but all led to dead ends. Theories abounded – that the children were taken overseas, handed to a religious sect, transported interstate. But the possibility that the children had been the victims of an undetected paedophile, operating in the local area, never gained much traction.

When Stuart first met Mostyn, he gave him the dossier of information he had gathered about Hank Harrison and his family. Included was a description of the man seen with the Beaumont children that day, which matched what we had found out about Hank. Mostyn took the dossier home to read, then contacted Stuart to set up another meeting. 'This is the best thing I have read on this case, period,' Moss said. 'No one has come near to finding out as much about someone who could have been involved.' He asked if he could get 'a second opinion' and show the information to Pieter Vogel, who also worked at Glenelg CIB on the original case.

Vogel is a sprightly gentleman in his 80s, who still speaks with a soft German accident. After World War II, he immigrated to Australia from Germany; as a teenager living in Berlin, his family hid his older brother from the Nazis because he'd deserted from the Russian front, then survived occupation by the Russian army. When he came to Australia in the 1950s, he tried a number of occupations before joining SAPOL.

Vogel came on duty at Glenelg the day after the Beaumonts' disappearance, when the case was still a missing persons investigation. 'A man was arrested at the beach and we locked him up for exposing himself,' Pieter remembered. 'He later came back and thanked us, because he couldn't be a suspect in the children's disappearance.' By the second night, however, the situation turned serious and it was feared the children may already have been murdered.

'People had dreams and premonitions [about the case],' Pieter recalled. 'One guy said he was Jesus Christ. Ron Blight asked the man where his beard was. "It's invisible," the man replied and we had to lock him up. A bloke said the children were buried under a driveway, but it was just a concrete slab. Croiset then came from Holland but he was a quack ... he first said they were buried under a block of flats, then at the Minda Home and lastly a warehouse. It was a circus.'

When we met with Pieter, he was impressed with the information Stuart had gathered about Hank Harrison. Hank, Vogel said, had never come to the notice of Glenelg CIB, but he remembered his son 'causing a bit of trouble'.

One thing had always troubled Vogel about the case. 'Paedophiles don't usually kill their victims,' he said. 'They groom them and abuse them over a long period of time. But a man with wealth and position in the community ... they would have a lot to lose if they were found out.'

We asked him whether police ever checked the backyards of local houses. 'We did a door knock, not a backyard search,' Pieter said. 'It's too easy to dispose of a body in South Australia ... Sandy soil, small packages that could have fit in a car ... they could have been buried in any backyard.'

Mostyn also recommended we speak to a former detective from SAPOL's Major Crime unit, whose name has been withheld in this book for privacy reasons. The Beaumont case, the detective told us, should have been treated as a homicide rather than a missing persons case. 'My attitude was, it was a homicide, straight away,' he said. 'I spoke to Ron Blight about it the next day and he said, "I think they're goners" ... that was the word he used. It was the only explanation. It was not as if they fell asleep in the seaweed and drifted off. But some ... maintained the view that if you don't have any bodies, there hasn't been a murder.'

Following the disappearance of the Beaumont children, policing changed in South Australia. If a case was declared a 'major crime', detectives would be seconded from the suburbs and operate from a suburban station. Major Crime investigations were conducted by small, decentralised units of detectives rather than falling upon the heads of under-resourced local detectives.

When Laurie Draper became police commissioner in the early 1970s, one of the first jobs he undertook was to allocate detectives to 'tidy up' the Beaumont files, to ensure all procedures and protocols had been followed correctly. If there was ever an inquiry into the investigation, SAPOL wanted 'all points covered'.

'There would have been some criticism of the department,' said the former detective sitting with us. 'Policing is the easiest job in the world to criticise ... you're forever looking over your shoulder. But there were certain aspects of the initial inquiry even I wasn't happy about.'

Detective Sergeants Ron 'Wings' Blight was given the first opportunity to go through the entire file at his own pace, and was offered as much help as he needed. 'Blighty said he couldn't go through that again,' the former detective told us. 'It had such a huge effect on his health.' John McCall later undertook a complete audit of the Beaumont case at the behest of Major Crime. Having been so involved in the Adelaide Oval abductions, if there were any links to the Beaumont disappearance other than circumstantial similarities, McCall never spoke about them publicly.

'From the very beginning [of the Adelaide Oval case], the talk was that we weren't looking for three bodies, but five,' said the ex-detective. 'Abducted from a crowded area, in broad daylight, with no bodies found, [the five children] would have to be together ... that was the talk.' In both cases, the children seemingly disappeared into thin air. 'There is a direct correlation between the randomness of the abductions and the organisation of the man responsible,' the former detective says. 'He was highly organised, and he would have had a "Plan B" in case something went wrong. The sheer guts of it ... But why did it stop? There was no thumbing his nose at the police and keeping going ... for some reason it all stopped.'

We showed the former detective our information about Hank Harrison. 'As a former investigator, it has red flags all over it,' he explained to us. 'The information you have collected would be reasonable to issue a general search warrant [on a known address]. I wouldn't have hesitated to issue one. You find the bodies of the children, it's all over.'

Our only information about the possible location of the bodies, according to Stuart's dossier, was Warwick Harrison's assertion that the bodies of the three children were in the sandpit at the family factory.

We had hit a brick wall and we needed advice. Where could we go, we asked, if SAPOL wouldn't investigate what we had found out?

'You could always take the information to the coroner and get him to resolve it,' the former detective said. 'You have a witness wanting to tell his story … he says he saw the children on the day they disappeared and his father was involved. Get him to tell his story on tape … shake the tree and then see what falls out.'

Chapter 15

The Beaumont Legacy

In 2005, filmmaker Graham McNeice was commissioned to make a series of documentaries about infamous Australian crimes. The following year, McNeice's production team contacted me and asked if I might act as a consultant for the programs on the Wanda Beach murders and the disappearance of the Beaumont children, which were being linked in a one-hour special. I said I would, as long as neither show promoted any one theory above the other. I provided the team with my file notes, contact numbers and newspaper clippings from the research I had gathered in writing books on both cases.

We filmed for four hours one morning and I effectively went right through both cases in chronological order. They edited this down to my best two-and-a-half minutes. When I watched the premiere of the double episode, I was amazed to find the producers had tacked on a 45-minute interview with an Adelaide family who were adamant their father had been involved in the disappearance of the children. A woman, her face pixellated, told how she had seen the bodies of the children in the boot of her father's car, their faces heavily made-up like marionette dolls.

The day after the show aired, Graham rang me to thank me for my assistance and asked how I liked the show. I told him it was fine, especially the Wanda episode, but I was disappointed he had included the interview with the woman at the end of the Beaumont program. In my opinion, it made the entire program look like it was set up to support her unchallenged claims, and undermined the documentary's objectivity.

The family had been persuasive, McNeice said, and their story was compelling. He had flown to Adelaide and personally interviewed a female member of the family for four hours and she never once deviated from her story. It was exactly the scenario we now found ourselves in with the Harrison family, although we chose to investigate the claims and give our information to SAPOL rather than going straight to the media. I thanked Graham for the opportunity to work on the episodes and wished him well.

When I spoke to SAPOL days later, they said they had investigated the woman's claims some years ago and ruled her father out as a suspect. Some time later, a lawyer in Adelaide sent me a court transcript of the woman's case against her father's estate. In SAPOL's view, there was little credence to her claims, and no charges were laid by police in relation to them.

Interestingly, when the *Crime Investigation Australia* program was repeated, as it is every January on the anniversary of the disappearance, the interview with the woman had been deleted from the program.

* * *

The disappearance of the three Beaumont children from Glenelg Beach has never been far from the national consciousness. The events of that hot summer's day in 1966 have become an integral part of Australia's urban mythology, a ready warning for the Baby Boomer generation about the dangers of talking to strangers. In the decades since, urban myths about the children have solidified into accepted 'fact' and different theories have been promoted in the media, but somehow the case still remains a mystery.

Many people haven't been able to grasp the implications of what really happened to the Beaumont children that day. To do so, one would have to imagine the unimaginable. Many still cling to the hope that the children are alive. The harsh reality is that they were most likely killed on the day they disappeared.

There have been other child abductions in Adelaide since, though none, not even the Adelaide Oval case, have had the same impact as the plight of the Beaumonts. On 3 January 1983, 10-year-old Louise Bell was snatched from her Hackham West home by an intruder, believed to have cut through a window fly-screen. Almost a decade later, on 7 October 1992, 12-year-old Rhianna Barreau left her Morphett Vale home and walked to the nearby Reynella shopping centre. Police believe she was abducted and murdered although, like Louise Bell, her body has never been found. Rewards have been posted for these cases, but they remain unsolved to this day.

Journalist Andrew Rule perhaps came closest to articulating the profound impact the Beaumont case has had, when he wrote that Australia continues to be 'mesmerised by a story as mysterious as *Picnic at Hanging Rock*, and as sinister as *Silence of the Lambs* ... It has been burned into the national psyche, transcending time and place in a way other crimes have not. It marks, perhaps, an end of innocence for an old Australia, when doors were left unlocked and kids went to the beach alone. The Beaumont children are as much a part of popular culture as Ned Kelly and Don Bradman ... names that echo down the years and have become part of our mythology.'

In the years since their kids went missing, Grant and Nancy Beaumont have been encouraged to move away from Glenelg, but refused. 'I can't in case the kiddies come home,' Nancy said early on, in a 1967 interview. 'You see, I'm waiting for them to come back here

... perhaps someone could drop them at the front gate. Wouldn't it be dreadful if I wasn't here?'

Mr and Mrs Beaumont did eventually sell their Somerton Park home, before separating and ending their marriage. The parents lived into their nineties, remaining in Glenelg, but declined to be interviewed by the media. In February 1990, Grant Beaumont gave an interview of sorts for the first time in more than two decades – the journalist did not identify himself when soliciting remarks regarding the Family Murders case. Mr Beaumont had to be treated for a stress-related illness when the article was published. That same year, *The News* published digitally altered photos to show what the three Beaumont children might look like if they were still alive, commissioning the Toronto Police Department to conduct the experiment. Canadian Bette Clarke, a world leader in photographic identification, 'aged' the photographs of the three Beaumont children using a computer. Mr and Mrs Beaumont attempted to stop the publication of the photos, the pictures caused a huge backlash against the newspaper.

As Adelaide journalist Tom Prior observed, the Beaumonts 'were loving parents and built their lives around Jane, Arnna and Grant. There were rotten things said at the time the children disappeared but, as I wrote then, not many parents would survive scrutiny as well as the Beaumonts, not many couples thrown suddenly into a blinding spotlight would prove to have as few things to hide. The Beaumonts were, and are, good people who made one tragic mistake. They thought they still lived in a decent world where it was safe to let children go to the beach alone.'

Since Gerard Croiset's death in 1980, other people, some claiming 'psychic powers', have weighed in on the case. In January 1985, a Perth woman told the *West Australian* that she believed the Beaumont children were alive and living in Kalgoorlie. In the late 1960s, she had lived in a railway camp called Reid near the SA border in the Nullarbor Desert. Three children who answered to the general description of the Beaumont children moved into the camp with their elderly parents in 1966, before moving to the WA gold town of Kalgoorlie. Perth CIB interviewed the woman, her husband and her son, and was able to track down the family in Geraldton, WA. Their name was Kilowsky and they definitely weren't Jane, Arnna and Grant Beaumont.

The following year, workmen at the West Torrens dump stumbled across a 'comprehensive file of annotated newspapers and newspaper clippings' related to the Beaumont case. The clippings were underlined in red pen with comments scrawled in the margins ... 'not in sandhills, in sewerage drain', 'she used to comb my hair', 'I understand', 'lies, all bluff' and 'no, no, no'. Police quickly established that the clippings had been dumped by the family of an elderly woman, who had spent years collecting news stories on the Beaumonts. When the woman died, her relatives had taken the file and some of her personal items to the local rubbish dump; there was nothing more to it.

In March 1990, 51-year-old Adelaide woman June Cox informed SAPOL that the Beaumont children, and Joanne Ratcliffe and Kirste Gordon, were 'calling her' from where their bodies were buried, in a paddock near Myponga Reservoir. The children had been 'speaking to her' for the past 11 years, she maintained, but only recently had she been able to pinpoint their remains. The media, of course, had just reported that Adelaide detectives were searching the Myponga Reservoir, in light of Mr B's revelations at the committal hearing of Bevan von Einem in the Family Murders Case.

Later in 1990, bones found in a Glenelg car yard in Brighton Road were originally thought to be human, but were later identified as animal bones. Then in 1992, SAPOL investigated claims that the Beaumont children's bodies were buried in a dam in Second Valley. These reports had initially been checked out in the late 1980s, after several different sources informed police that the bodies of the Beaumont children could have been dumped there. But SAPOL confirmed that local farmers used the dam to dispose of sheep carcasses, and no evidence relating to the Beaumont case was found.

In April 2004, a New Zealand man sparked a media frenzy; he told an Australian woman that, when he was growing up in Dunedin on the South Island, his mother believed they had been living next door to the Beaumont children. A shop assistant overheard the conversation and reported it to the local police. Within days, a member of that neighbouring family, 47-year-old Judith Hewitt (nee Larson), was located in a Dunedin boarding home. Hewitt volunteered the necessary information about her childhood, and the matter was quickly cleared up.

In 2006, media clairvoyant Scott Russell Hill told *Woman's Day* magazine that he knew where the Beaumont children were buried. He said he had been able to solve the mystery because the children had guided him 'from the other side'. Scott Russell Hill wrote that he knew the identity of two key suspects – one of whom was known to Jane. 'Jane would never have gone with somebody she didn't know,' he said.

According to Hill's book, *Psychic Detective*, that claim brought a knock on the door from Detective Inspector Brian Swan in 2007. Hill wrote that Swan told him about the difficulty of digging up backyards so many decades after the fact. 'Say you live at, for example, 21 Smith Street, and I knock on your door and say, "Hello, I'm Brian Swan from the South Australia Police and we have information that the Beaumont children are buried in your backyard." How would you react to that?'

In January 2012, just before the 46th anniversary of the Beaumont children's disappearance, a David Estes of Irvine, Kentucky in the USA told news outlets he 'thought he might be Grant Beaumont'. The claim was based solely on photographs of Estes as a small child and because he 'felt no relation to other members of his family'. Estes' bizarre story was picked up when he stated that local police and SAPOL had taken him seriously. He claimed that a friend of his father made a deathbed confession to him, that his father had 'once drunkenly confessed to abducting him from hospital'. Estes' own mother dismissed the claims, and when he refused to take a DNA test (because it would cost $10,000 to perform), the story was finally dismissed.

There is an old police saying that 'a case often dies with the detective investigating it'. This is because, traditionally, detectives were allowed to keep copies of case notes, files and photos from the investigations in which they served. Many of the detectives who worked on the Beaumont case have since died, taking with them peripheral understandings of the original investigation, but sometimes the thoughts of the investigating police came to light.

In 1990, former homicide squad detective Jack Zeurnet confirmed to the media that Adelaide detectives had investigated the existence of a US-based religious sect in the Adelaide Hills during the late 1960s and early 1970s. Zeurnet said that police had traced the sect to a home in Alberton, but lost track of it in Western Australia. Zeurnet believed that, because the Beaumont case did not 'follow the usual pattern of sex killings', the involvement of a sect 'carried some weight' for a time, but this line of investigation was eventually abandoned.

Then, in 1996, the family of the late Geoffrey Leane, the former Deputy Commissioner of Police, showed their father's diaries to the *Adelaide Advertiser*. Based on his diaries, Leane believed that the children's bodies were dumped in a shipping container, which was lying unclaimed in a foreign port. Leane did not go public with his beliefs while he was alive, although he did brief Premier Frank Walsh. The assertions were quickly dismissed, because no foreign port had reported such a find.

After his retirement, Stan Swaine raised or promoted various theories about the Beaumonts: that they were taken by a former mental patient into the Mount Lofty Ranges; that they were handed over to a religious cult by their parents and were still alive; and finally, that they were abducted, murdered and buried anonymously in Brighton Cemetery.

In 1997, Swaine declared that he had 'found Jane Beaumont' living in Canberra. The 41-year-old woman, who allegedly shared the eldest Beaumont girl's birthday (10 September, 1956) and had 'some of the same characteristics' as the missing girl, had volunteered to medical authorities that she was 'Jane' three years earlier. Swaine, who was staying in the nation's capital with his daughter, came into contact with the woman and rushed into the media with his new theory. The woman declined to go public with her claims. Swaine wanted her to provide a fingerprint sample and match it against Jane Beaumont's schoolbooks, which he knew were still in SAPOL's possession. The woman applied to have a restraining order served on Swaine and her former therapist, before going into hiding. SAPOL dismissed the claims after checking official records in Canberra and tracking down her parents, who supplied a copy of the woman's birth certificate.

In 2001, Swaine still believed there was a 'strong possibility' that the children were alive. He apparently had a new theory, but the media and his former colleagues had stopped listening. One of the last conversations he had with his estranged children, shortly before his death, was when he told one of his adult daughters from his hospital bed: 'This is going to be big. I will solve it.'

During the course of researching this book, we learned of another scenario that was investigated by SAPOL. Former detectives have intimated that SAPOL investigated an allegation that the Beaumont children were abducted from Glenelg by ferry and taken to Kangaroo Island, 200 kilometres away. It would likely be safe to assume that SAPOL had solid information on which to act – perhaps members of the public, writers or journalists brought forward claims that needed further investigation. Presumably the claims were dismissed.

Today, information that leads to the conviction of the person or persons responsible for the disappearance of the Beaumont children, or of Joanne Ratcliffe and Kirste Gordon, carries a reward of $200,000. Only two crimes have higher rewards – the 1994 National Crime Authority bombing, which killed Detective Sergeant Geoffrey Bowen and seriously injured lawyer Peter Wallis, and the unsolved murders of the four young men linked to the Family Murders.

Chapter 16

The Thin Blue Line

As a former British serviceman, Commonwealth Policeman, South Australia Police detective and insurance fraud investigator, Bill Hayes has had decades of personal and professional experience in dealing with frauds, criminals and the seriously deranged.

Hayes first came to Australia while serving as a paratrooper with the British Armed Forces, in the late 1960s. Born in Northern Ireland, he served in the Middle East, the Far East and even his homeland during 'the troubles'. His Irish accent has disappeared over the years, which he attributes to living in England from a young age and becoming a merchant seaman at age 15.

When Bill eventually left the British forces, he found it difficult to adjust to civilian life. 'I was going to join the Australian armed forces,' he told us. 'I thought that they would be serving overseas, but they weren't and I got talked out of it. Someone suggested joining the Australian Federal Police, the Commonwealth Police as they were known then.

'I was based in Woomera, in South Australia, and I enjoyed working with SAPOL on a number of investigations, and so I decided to join them. The culture was close to military, because we had a former brigadier [John McKinna] as our commissioner for many years. We had a 'service' type culture and camaraderie, really ... [we would] stand together and get the job done.

'We were a police force in a small state, with some incredibly good officers and detectives, who were inspiring in many ways in how they went about their work. For a small state, they were very effective, because we really did have some serious crimes in the 1970s.'

I asked if some of the crimes committed in Adelaide over the years had surprised him. 'I am no more or less surprised than anyone else, although we do tend to have bizarre murders involving young people – Truro, the Family Murders and Snowtown, as well as the disappearance of children like the Beaumonts, the Gordon and Ratcliffe children and others, for example. Having my background in the armed forces, death and murder didn't surprise me too much. I had seen the worst that humans can do to each other, so it was not a huge culture shock for me. That's why I advanced quickly into the Criminal Investigation Branch.'

During Bill's time with SAPOL, it changed its system from compiling running sheets to a major crime plan that was centred on computer technology. It was 'a huge revolution in how major crime was investigated,' Bill said, 'although the computerised system was a far more scientific approach.' Policing had, until then, been based on the old-fashioned network of information that all police services relied on.

'The Special Crime Squad, now disbanded, like the Major Crime Squad, had been based on that,' remembered Bill. 'Our job was to target known criminals and see what they were up to and we worked with the Bureau of Criminal Intelligence (BCI) at SAPOL to dig up information and links to crimes committed or being planned, or the activities of known criminals. We would use our massive network of informants that we had cultivated over long periods of time to launch investigations and determine just who was involved and in what.'

We asked Bill what he knew about the Beaumont case before he was contacted by Stuart. 'I had been fortunate to have had a look at some of the statements in the Beaumont case when I was a detective in SAPOL,' he remembered. 'I was at a loose end for a couple of days and I was put into a room with a pile of boxes containing statements, etc, from the Beaumont case, to familiarise myself with the original investigation. SAPOL will often do that, to get a look with a fresh set of eyes in unsolved cases. I had no preconceived ideas about the case because I wasn't in Australia when it happened, but I believed that whoever took the children was not a known paedophile.

'If he had been a known offender,' Bill went on, 'given the intensity of the investigation over many years, with the information coming in at the time and the public interest – let alone the police interest – something would have turned up.'

Was he happy with the way the case had been conducted, I asked, given the technical limitations of the time?

'I didn't see anything in the original police statements that was any different to what we were doing in the 1980s,' he said, 'bearing in mind that thousands of statements were taken, and I believe SAPOL did a tremendous job under the circumstances and given the availability of their resources at the time.'

We also asked what he thought was working against police in this case. 'The fact that the person involved was not known to police in any criminal way,' he answered immediately. 'Also the manner in which the children disappeared ... they weren't taken kicking and screaming off the street, it appears they went willingly with the man seen with them at the Colley Reserve ... and, of course, the fact they disappeared without a trace. In that regard it was very difficult for the police to even know where to start. They obviously cast a huge net to see what they could find, but it didn't work.' Without a crime scene, forensic evidence or a suspect, the police were really up against it.

'What really intrigued me was the £1 note the children used to buy their lunch,' Bill added. 'The £1 note was a substantial sum of money at the time … and to buy pies and pasties with it was the key for me. Who gave them the pound note?'

An opportunity came up with the State Government Insurance Commission and Bill applied for a job as an insurance investigator there. He then became a private investigator, specialising in insurance fraud, but engaging in other complex investigations. He draws the line at investigating domestic issues – an errant wife, a husband having an affair – and, with a Masters in Business Administration, has a long list of corporate clients.

Ninety-nine times out of 100, if someone rang Bill about the Beaumont children, he would have rolled his eyes and said, 'Here we go again.' Over the years, because there are so few known facts about the crime, the media have tended to run with any theory, no matter how improbable, and Bill was sceptical. Except this time, because Mostyn Matters was involved, Bill listened to Stuart.

'I knew that if Mostyn felt it worthwhile to recommend my involvement, then it was worth looking at,' he said. 'Moss had been part of the investigation into the event when it occurred. He is a man of great reputation and integrity and someone for whom I have the greatest regard and respect. Stuart had done as much as a private person could do, and he realised he needed professional assistance to take the case any further.'

Bill deliberately left the door of his office open when he invited Stuart to sit down. Stuart showed him the dossier he'd put together on Hank Harrison, and systematically went through the major points that implicated the deceased businessman in the disappearance of the children. Bill Hayes flicked through the dossier as he listened intently, before reaching across his desk, picking up the phone and talking to his receptionist. 'Hold my meetings for the rest of the day,' he said. As he got up and closed the door, Bill told Stuart this new information 'was very interesting and needs to be seriously looked at.'

'I started off wanting to prove that everything Stuart was saying was wrong,' Bill admitted. 'I looked at the information he had gathered with the same view as I would have with any criminal investigation, because that's what would happen if it was ever taken before a court of law. I did that to cover all bases and so that any evidence that might exist would stand up if needed.'

The most important piece of information Stuart had was a name – someone to investigate with a view to ruling them in or out of the inquiry, standard police procedure.

'I told Stuart that if I agreed to do this, I wasn't going to become obsessed about solving the case,' Bill said. 'As an investigator, my concern was whether there was any truth in what was being said about Hank and if there was any evidence to support it or the contrary.' Bill knew officers who had worked on the case and become obsessed with it. They wanted to be the one to solve the mystery – sometimes for the family, sometimes for themselves. 'I was determined not to be another of those,' he said frankly. 'I told Stuart I wouldn't be accepting anything he said on face value … if evidence supported the view that there was nothing to what Warwick was alleging about his father, I would be upfront and tell him that straight away.'

Bill was going off on holiday and had a lot of free time to read and re-read the information in the dossier and my 2006 book. 'I came back to work with a fair deal of knowledge about what Stuart had found out with his inquiries and it was very interesting … There was a spark there in me, this really had legs.'

I was interested to know what exactly in the dossier provided that spark. 'The purse Stuart saw at Hank's house – it could have been the key to the whole case,' said Bill. 'It's well-known that some killers keep a 'trophy' of a kill – that really got me concerned. It wasn't

Stuart's fault that he couldn't get the purse out of the house so that it could be shown to the parents and tested ... That's when I think he realised he needed a professional's help.'

I asked Bill what he would have done in the circumstances. 'I would have considered calling the police and trying to convince them to seize the purse,' he told me. 'I may have even considered pocketing it and getting it the hell out of there, and taken my chances with a misdemeanour theft, but I would have been concerned as to what doing this might have done to the case, if there was to be one. The end may have justified the means, but if I have difficulty deciding what to do now, how hard would it have been for someone like Stuart to make that decision on the spot?'

There are so many unanswered questions about that purse, Bill went on. 'It certainly was a missed opportunity. What did the woman do with it? Where did it come from, why was it there and where did it go? Norma had inherited perhaps millions, but said that she went out to an op shop and bought a 1960s-style child's purse, then put it in a place in the house where no one goes and where Hank kept his stuff? And then she tells the police she threw it out when he asks her for it? It doesn't make sense ...'

Stuart's dossier flagged a number of issues that raised Bill's antennae. 'Look where Hank was living,' Bill pointed out. 'It had always been in my mind that wherever the Beaumonts went after being at the reserve, it wasn't that far away. If the children were compliant with their kidnapper, they could then be driven anywhere. They weren't noticed because there were possibly dozens of kids hopping into and out of cars with their parents in Glenelg that day and it certainly wouldn't have been out of the ordinary to the casual observer. Proximity to a house perhaps made it easier for the man ...

'The oldest child Jane was seen as a fighter ... she would have protected the kiddies with her life, and possibly did so ... so she would not have gone quietly when things started to happen. That intrigued me as well.'

Bill hadn't seen anything like Stuart's dossier when he reviewed the original case files in the 1970s; he described it as 'the best new information about the case that I have seen or heard about'. After spending five minutes with Stuart, Bill could tell he wasn't 'some wacko with an agenda ... here was a serious, sane person with some information that needed to be looked at.'

To the best of his knowledge, nobody had ever given tangible evidence about the fate of the Beaumont children that later turned out to be accurate. Yet here we had a family member, who told a writer what she knew, and it had been thoroughly researched by Stuart. 'It was, in my opinion, too compelling to simply ignore.'

SAPOL's apparent reluctance to investigate the information was understandable, Bill explained. The Major Crime squad would have all sorts of "whackos" trying to solve crimes for them. Ninety-nine percent of them are time-wasters, and the police just don't have the time to deal with everyone who has a new 'theory' based on something they dreamed or whatever.

'I remember a fellow came into SAPOL and wanted me to provide him with a piece of a victim's clothing, so he could get "vibrations" from the material ... I have also had some wonderful, well-meaning people who have tried to help, but they tend to get lumped in the same basket as the "wackos."'

But Bill Hayes also presented us with a statistic – that 90 percent of crimes are solved by information provided by the public. 'It's very rare you get the Sherlock Holmes-type investigation solving cases. Information from the public clears up most crimes ... little snippets of secondary, circumstantial or peripheral evidence that are put together to form a somewhat compelling case for the skilled police investigator to use to solve a crime.

'I also work on the theory of synchronicity, which purports that events are often running parallel to each other, without either party knowing about the other at the time – but then, for some reason and at some point in time, they converge and start to make sense. I find life is like that, especially in investigations.'

If the man was active in paedophile or criminal circles, said Bill, he would have been given up by someone years ago. 'Bearing in mind, there were "decent criminals" in the past who had families themselves and would have been repulsed by his behaviour … if they had known about him.'

Bill was very interested in what Stuart had discovered about Hank's 'habits', such as his giving out £1 notes, his demeanour with children and how he conducted his private life in regard to his satin fetish, and seemed to feel that it was too damn close to dismiss. His recommendation was to find where Warwick was living now and to speak with him 'on the record'.

Above: The Paringa Park warehouse in Somerton Park where Dutch clairvoyant Gerard Croiset said the children were 'accidentally buried' in 1966. The warehouse was demolished in 2007, but no trace of the children was ever found.

Left: Workmen excavate part of the Paringa Park warehouse floor in 1967. Despite the efforts of businessman Con Polites and various citizens committees, the search was based on nothing more than a hunch.

Above: The search for the missing Beaumont children was one of the most extensive in Australia.

Right: The first sketch of the suspect seen playing with the children on the beach the day they disappeared.

Left: Bevan von Einem was found guilty of the 1983 murder of 15-year-old Richard Kelvin and implicated in the unsolved murders of several other young men in the late 1970s and early 1980s.

Below: A statue of Captain William Light, the founder of Adelaide, points to Adelaide Oval, where the city's 'forgotten crime' occurred in August 1973.

Left: An artist's sketch of the man seen carrying Kirste Gordon out of Adelaide Oval in August 1973, with Joanne Ratcliffe following them both. This man resembled the Beaumont suspect from 1966, but who was it?

Below: The grandstand and shed area of the Adelaide Oval where two young girls were snatched by a man in August 1973.

Joanne Ratcliffe (*above*) was
abducted from Adelaide Oval on
25 August 1973, aged nine years
old. Ratcliffe had taken four-
year-old Kirste Gordon (*opposite*)
to the toilet during a local
Aussie Rules game, when they
disappeared.

Above: Colourful Glenelg in the early 2000s, with shops still showing the 'Polites' signs, honouring the memory of the late real estate tycoon Con Polites.

Below: Former Detective Mostyn Matters (left) and postman Tom Patterson (right), pictured together in Glenelg in 2008.

Above: 'Warwick', the son of the 'Satin Man' (left) lunching with a family friend (second from left), former Glenelg detective Mostyn Matters (second from right) and co-author Stuart Mullins (right) in North Queensland in late 2014. Rather than hide from his allegations, Warwick Harrison was happy that his story had been told and was looking forward to the future and good health. He died in 2015 without ever being formally interviewed by SAPOL.

Right: A sample of the satin pyjamas taken from Hank Harrison's Glenelg home by a removalist and told to 'get rid of' by Hank's second wife. This photo was sent to the authors in 2013.

Left: The cover of 'Little Women', imprint date 1960, found in a Glenelg op shop by co-author Stuart Mullins.

Below: In 2014 SAPOL undertook a partial dig of a factory in suburban Adelaide, but nothing was found. Police were later criticised by the media for not digging deep enough, or extensively enough, nor having the citizens who came forward with information on hand. (Photo courtesy Channel 7)

Chapter 17

The 'Postie'

When Stuart and I met with Peter Woite, at the time the Head of Major Crime, and Detective Inspector Brian Swan, at the SAPOL offices in June 2005, they declined to provide us with the original case files, partly because they knew we would contact the original witnesses. They were correct. When I wrote my 2003 book about the Wanda Beach murders, cold case detectives had provided me with original case files and I re-interviewed key witnesses 37 years later. Many police organisations have since tightened access to cold case files. Many of the elderly witnesses to the Beaumonts' disappearance had passed away, but I would have liked to interview the teenage girl sitting with her grandparents at Colley Reserve.

Instead, Brian Swan provided us with a hand-typed, two-page summary of the case, called a resume in police parlance. Given that the files for the Beaumont case had been completely computerised in the 1980s, the resume struck me as anachronistic – it looked like a tenth-generation photocopy and contained a number of errors. Swan also provided a photocopy of a photo, reproduced in this book, of the place where the children were last seen, playing with the man on Colley Reserve, a grassy area on the north side of Holdfast Bay Sailing Club, at Glenelg Beach.

We have recorded the entire resume here:

Resume of the investigation into the abduction of the three BEAUMONT children missing from Glenelg Beach, South Australia, since the 26th of January, 1966

On Wednesday the 26th of January 1966, three children, Jane BEAUMONT aged 9 years, Arnna BEAUMONT aged 7 years, and Grant BEAUMONT aged 4 years, disappeared from the Glenelg foreshore, Adelaide, South Australia. Despite extensive Police enquiries, they have not been seen or heard of since.

BACKGROUND

The BEAUMONT family consisted of Mr. Beaumont, who at the time of the disappearance was a middle-aged travelling salesman, ex-taxi driver, Mrs. Beaumont, also middle-aged, who performed home duties, and their three children. The two eldest children attended a local primary school. It was apparently common for Mrs. Beaumont to allow the three children to go to the beach together. The eldest child Jane was apparently very 'grown-up' and 'motherly' towards the two younger children. The children were apparently generally well behaved, had been instructed not to speak to strangers, and got along well with each other. The Beaumont family lived in a typical suburban home less than three kilometres from the beach.

EVENTS OF 26/1/66.

The 26th of January is Australia Day, usually associated with a public holiday. The 26th of January 1966, however, fell on a Wednesday, therefore the holiday was taken at a later time. At this time of the year however all schools in South Australia were on school holidays. January is also mid-summer in Australia, and on the 26th of Jan. '66 the weather in Adelaide was hot, clear, with a light breeze. High tide was around

12.30p.m. It has been established that the events of this day leading up to the disappearance of the three children were as follows:

0945 hrs – Mrs. Beaumont allows the three children to walk the short distance to the bus stop. She understood that they were going to the Glenelg Beach for the day, and would return home on the bus at about noon.

1000 hrs – Bus driver recalls collecting the three children. Although he cannot recall them getting off the bus, He [sic] round finished in Moseley St. Glenelg, a short distance from the beach. Another passenger also recalls seeing the children on the bus.

1015 hrs – The children are seen by the local postman walking along Jetty Road Glenelg towards the beach.

1100 hrs – The children are seen sitting on a section of lawn alongside the Holdfast Bay sailing club, overlooking the beach, by a school friend of Jane. This person does not speak to Jane.

1200 hrs – Between 1100 hrs and 1200 hrs, several persons recall seeing the children on this same section of lawn. They also recall seeing the suspect either talking or playing with the children. At 1145 hrs the children are known to have attended at a local cake shop and purchased food, including extra food other than what they would have eaten. The children paid for this food using money other than what their mother had provided them with. It would appear that the children also purchased food for the suspect, using money provided by him.

The children were last seen at about 1200 hours on that day. It is believed that the male person seen talking and playing with the children, between 1100 hours and 1200 hours, may be responsible for their disappearance. No mode of travel is known for this person.

The three missing children are described as follows:

Jane Nararlie [sic] BEAUMONT: born 10/9/56. 4'6" tall, with fair ear-length sun-bleached hair with a pushed-back fringe at the front. She may have been wearing a tortoiseshell hair band with a yellow ribbon in her hair. She had hazel eyes, a thin face, thin build, and had freckles. At the time of her disappearance she was wearing light green shorts, canvas tartan pattern sandshoes with white soles. She was carrying an airways type bag (possibly blue) containing three towels, a book titled 'Little Women', and a white money purse containing eight shillings and sixpence. She was well-spoken, but stuttered when excited. Her two front teeth were prominent.

Arnna Kathleen BEAUMONT: born 11/11/58, 4' tall, with dark brown hair with a fringe. She had dark brown eyes, suntanned complexion, and plump build. She was wearing tan shorts over red and white striped bathers. She was also wearing tan coloured sandals.

Grant Ellis BEAUMONT: born 12/7/61, 3' tall, with short brown hair with a fringe. He had brown eyes, olive complexion, very suntanned, thin build. He was wearing green swimming trunks with vertical white stripes, under green cotton shorts. He was also wearing red leather type sandals.

The male person seen talking and playing with the Beaumont children immediately prior to their disappearance is described as follows:

Male, mid to late 30s, about 6' tall, thin to athletic build, with light brown short hair swept back and parted on the left side, clean-shaven, suntanned complexion, with a thin face. Australian accent. Wearing blue bathers with a single white stripe down the outside of each leg.

There are a few points to note regarding this brief summary. Firstly, Jane Beaumont's middle name is incorrect; her mother named her Jane Nartare, an unusual middle name derived from the Latin word for 'water sports'. The irony of the name was not lost on detectives, given Jane loved the water and ultimately disappeared from a public beach.

Secondly, the timing of postman Tom Patterson's sighting was in dispute for many years; it was thought he might have seen the children at the end of his postal run, in the afternoon. Swan later confirmed to me that, when he took over the case in 1988, he interviewed all the main witnesses again and Patterson said the sighting was in the morning.

Lastly, it was well known that the colour of the local surf club was navy blue, with the club insignia stitched on the side. Brian Swan later confirmed in an email to me that the bathers the man seen playing with the Beaumonts was wearing were sky blue with a white stripe.

So many questions remained: was the man a local resident or a tourist travelling through Adelaide? Where was his carry bag, car keys or car? Did he walk to the beach? Why did he get changed at the beach if he lived locally?

I had previously written a book on the unsolved Wanda Beach murders (*Wanda: The Untold Story*, 2004). A woman who read the book contacted me and told me of a Sydney surf lifesaver who allegedly moved to Adelaide at the end of 1965, after boarding with her family. The man was obsessed with knives and young girls. I gave Brian Swan the man's name, being careful to spell his distinctive last name, but it failed to receive a 'hit' when entered into the computer system.

'What if the person responsible for the Beaumont children's disappearance, or the Wanda case for that matter, was not known to police?' I asked. Such a person would not be in the computer system, Swan told me. Obviously, the computer could only cross-check evidence with known people.

When I returned to Sydney, I told the woman who had contacted me that I'd reported the man to SAPOL, but there was nothing in their system. Soon after, I received a package from the woman. Inside was a blue Trans Australia Airways shoulder bag, which had been left in her house after the man returned to live with her family in the 1970s. She noted there appeared to be a bloodstain on the inside of the bag, near the zipper.

This was intriguing. *Searching for the Beaumont Children* had not been published yet and the significance of the children's carry bag was not widely known. I contacted Swan again and mailed the bag to them. He told me that he went through the entire Beaumont file, that there was no mention of the words 'TAA' on the airways bag, and that Mr and Mrs Beaumont again confirmed that their children had taken a blue, generic 'airways-type' bag to the beach. He had also examined the 'bloodstain' on the inside of the bag, which turned out to be a melted lolly.

I thanked Swan again, and said I hoped I hadn't wasted his time. He told me he received three or four calls a month about the case and always followed them up. A person would ring the Major Crime Squad with a new 'lead' – the name of a man selling ice-creams and drinks on the beach that day, for example – and he would investigate it. 'I'll contact the person who forwarded it and take it from there,' he said.

When *Searching for the Beaumont Children* was published, I sent him a copy. He said he put it in the SAPOL 'library', where the police keep a number of publications about certain crimes. I later wrote a book about Derek Percy (*Derek Percy: Australian Psycho*, 2008), the child murderer and longest-serving Victorian prisoner, who had been linked at one point to the Beaumont case. When I appeared on *Crime Investigation Australia* in 2007, Swan told me I was quickly becoming the 'go-to guy' on the Beaumont case, a role I never wanted or sought.

* * *

During one of their many conversations together, Mostyn Matters told Stuart that he personally knew the postman, Tom Patterson, who had seen the children the day they disappeared, and offered to introduce Stuart. They eventually met for coffee in 2007. Then aged in his late 80s, Tom Patterson was a kind-hearted, softly spoken gentleman who had vivid memories of the three Beaumont children. In the 1960s, the 'postie', as most people called him, would deliver the mail twice a day via bicycle. 'You got to know your local postie by name,' Stuart recalled. 'As an era, the 1960s was a much less rushed time, and it wasn't unusual at all to see the baker or the fruit and veg van in your street every day. The "milkie" even delivered your pint of bottled milk to your doorstep. They delivered their goods, lived in the local area and watched the neighbourhood kids grow up.'

Tom started as a postman in 1934, but was put off during the Depression years. He then joined the armed services, where he saw active duty. He returned to his mail route in 1955 and was stationed at Glenelg Post Office, not far from the police station where Mostyn worked. Tom delivered the mail in Somerton Park for the next 34 years before retiring. Needless to say, he was a very fit man, having to cycle 20 to 30 kilometres every day – rain, hail or shine. 'The post must be delivered,' Tom laughed.

Tom had clear memories of Jane, Arnna and Grant Beaumont. 'They were always happy, smiling, energetic,' he recalled. When he delivered the post to their home, they would come running out to take the mail from him, calling, 'It's the postie!' Tom was to hear that call again on 26 January 1966, in Jetty Road, Glenelg – the last time he saw the children.

'Jane looked over Arnna and Grant and you could see she was a caring type of girl,' Tom said. 'She always had the time to say hello.' He remembered them as well-mannered kids, but most of all, always smiling. 'When you see children smiling and happy, you know it is a credit to the parents. Mr and Mrs Beaumont were devoted to their children.'

Tom dismissed out of hand any idea that the parents might have been involved in their children's disappearance. Tom knew Mr and Mrs Beaumont well, and described them as loving, caring parents. At the time, it was not unusual at all for children to go to the beach without their parents; children would walk miles to the beach and back then, in complete safety. Children enjoyed a freedom that has steadily vanished over the years.

Tom Patterson remembered that day in 1966 as 'hot, humid and very crowded'. He saw the children as they waved to him and heard them call out to him. There is no question that he saw them, but Tom was originally not quite sure when; was it in the morning or the afternoon? Police believe it was mid-morning, after the children hopped off the bus. Tom believes the sighting was closer to midday, but if true, that would only confirm what police already knew – that the children walked to Wenzel's cakes at midday to buy their lunch. Tom didn't see them with any man or other adult.

'There's not a week that goes by that I don't think about their smiling faces,' Tom told Stuart when they met. 'They shone.'

Tom Patterson lived in an aged care centre in Adelaide before passing away peacefully in 2014. His health deteriorated after the death of his beloved wife a few years ago, but his children visited him regularly and he was comfortable in his memories of a long and happy life.

At a time when Stuart was discovering the worst of what people can do to each other, meeting Tom Patterson reaffirmed his faith in human nature. 'Tom was a lovely guy to talk to, with his heart in the right place,' Stuart recalled. 'He had wonderful memories of a simpler time, when you knew the local people in the community ... and of the Beaumont children and their "happy shiny faces".'

Chapter 18

The Sins of the Father

Two years after Amanda Harrison first contacted us, private investigator Bill Hayes went to Queensland to interview her former husband, Warwick. 'He was living in a communal support house for men battling addiction at the time and he appeared to have been drinking and on his medication,' Bill Hayes told me later.

'His room was a mess and Amanda, who had come with me, helped clean it up. We sat in a common area, which wasn't the best place to talk, so we agreed to travel to the unit that Warwick was still renting, where we could speak privately. I realised that I was dealing with a person who was quite fragile in a mental sense and had been severely damaged by what had happened in his life.'

Bill felt that Warwick wanted to talk. 'We talked about Adelaide and house prices, he had a coffee and a smoke, and then we started talking about his deceased father Hank, and his links to the Beaumont children. Warwick answered quite spontaneously over the next two hours … We had a number of breaks and chatted normally – quite relaxed and friendly – but he told me essentially the same story he told Stuart some months before. I was quite impressed with him in many ways.'

Considering the number of interviews Bill has conducted over the years, he is particularly sensitive to people who are lying or making up a story as they go along. 'I watch what they do, what they say and how they say it,' Bill said. 'Warwick was telling the truth, as he knew it.'

Warwick, then in his fifties, had no objections to doing the interview with Bill or having the audio recorded. He described himself as 'semi-retired' and confirmed that he was originally from Glenelg, and had resided in the family home there for the first 20 years of his life. The conversation then proceeded as follows.

Bill: Can you give me a physical description of your father on or around the mid-1960s?

Warwick: Tall, lanky ... he was in the region of six foot, six-foot-one. In the early days he was blondish, but as he got older it turned darker and then to grey.

Bill: What would his hair colouring and hair have been like in – in about 1966?

Warwick: Maybe a slight wave ... fair colour.

Bill: Would he spend time down at the beach at all?

Warwick: In the water at Somerton Park and Glenelg, he'd be rubbing the girls up and down in front of his body. I'd think, 'you dirty old bastard'. He often took walks on his own. He was very much unto himself and we were very hesitant to ask him what he was doing. He was not a character that'd tell you where he was or what he was doing.

Bill: Was he a successful businessman?

Warwick: No, he nearly failed in his business in the early 1960s, and he had to bring in creditors to support him and jack up the business. Initially he started with the locals [as backers] and then, because he got in so much financial trouble, he had to go to the overseas people. He dealt with 'heavy people' but he seemed to thrive on it.

Bill: In what way?

Warwick: He could be very violent, extremely violent. He never went anywhere without a pistol … .38 police revolver. I think he felt he was inadequate and also it gave him a – a sense of superiority.

Bill: What was his childhood like?

Warwick: It was fucked up. His mother dressed him as a girl until he was five years of age, told him he was a girl and he just carried it on. She wanted a girl that much she decided to dress him in little girls' outfits … He admitted to me on many occasions that he had a straight-up fetish for women's clothing and, in particular, his mother made him little gowns of satin and he acquired this fetish for satin. It fitted his body exactly and rubbed against his skin, and it became quite sexually adequate for him to wear the gowns until he ejaculated.

Bill: He would become excited?

Warwick: He had a workshop and there was a big x-ray cabinet that my grandfather had built and he'd stash it full of dresses and he'd get dressed up. He'd shoot up the stairs and we used to be able to watch him. We had a laundry with a copper tub and I used to be able to hide in there and watch what he was doing.

I must have started watching him at about seven years of age. When my grandmother died, I was looking around and I found some of his clothing. My mother came out and said, 'Oh, you've found out the secret at last …' That was when I was about nine years of age and she said, 'Thank God you've finally found out.'

I just knew he was getting off on dresses and … these bloody satin outfits. I think his mother encouraged it. I think she made him the outfits and dresses and encouraged him to be a girl and mix with girls – his mother was 'sick'.

Bill: We had a conversation before when you told me that your father had sexually abused you?

Warwick: Violently, from the age of two years old. I've accepted it as I've got older. I've mentioned it to several psychiatrists and I've had sessions with a psychologist to overcome it.

Bill: What you're recalling now is basically what happened ... it's not something you made up?

Warwick: No, it's not delusional.

Bill: How long did this abuse go on for?

Warwick: Until I was 14 years of age ... I became big enough and strong enough to protect myself. One night he picked up a plate of food and slammed it into Mum's face and the china plate broke and cut her. I grabbed him by the hair and dragged him out in the passage and dropped him and I just held him down by his shoulders and punched the shit out of him and said, 'Don't you ever hit my mother again.' He left in his Pontiac and didn't come back for about four or five days.

Bill: He left you alone after that?

Warwick: He never hit my mother again. Never touched me again.

Bill: Were you afraid of your father?

Warwick: Terrified. Gut scared. He had weapons all over the house. But as I grew older, I thought he was pathetic. Hank was obviously a person who had fetishes ... a satin fetish. He was also very quick tempered ... I was glad to see the bastard prick buried.

Bill: If he was going to be found out, what would his reaction have been?

Warwick: He'd kill 'em. He wouldn't be found out. No doubt about it. He had no conscience. See, this is his illness. This is his precious illness, which he covets and loves, and he has an excuse for and it gives him an excuse to protect it no matter what. He told me that with money you can buy anyone.

I don't think he had any sexual relationship with my mother at all. He used to sneak off to the other bedroom so he could go to sleep in his pyjamas that were made of satin. I used to listen to him ... the slip, slip, slip, slip, slip ... of the satin.

Bill: Do you recall the conversation with Amanda when you saw the Beaumont TV program?

Warwick: That would have just flashed me back and I would have said something to her because we were fairly close and I didn't keep anything a secret from her so ... yeah, I would have said something to her.

Bill: Do you recall Australia Day 1966, January 26th, when the Beaumont children disappeared?

Warwick: I fully expected that the police would resolve the situation. I thought we had an adequate police force to resolve this, I didn't think it would go this far to be quite honest with you because it was three kids, like, you just don't lose them, you know, it doesn't happen.

Bill: Do you know anything about this?

Warwick: I saw them come into the backyard from the – the cubby-house. They came into the backyard, they came into dad's car, I think they were inside the house and that's it.

Bill: Where were you that day before you went to the cubby-house? Were you at home or away?

Warwick: I was at the bowling alley. I was working there ... I was a pin boy. I got home before lunch, I guess it was about – between 12 and 12.30. We used to get bits of bloody grass and roll-up cigarettes and all that sort of stuff, lawn-cuttings. Jeez, it used to make us cough. I think a friend was with me ... he couldn't stand my father, except when he gave us money to piss off. Around this time I saw three kids come into the backyard. Little kids, one's a little bit shorter than the rest, with short haircuts ... I think they had beach towels. I thought it was three girls, but the smallest one was a boy ... they looked lost.

Bill: Did you hear Hank talking to them?

Warwick: Yeah, I heard them talking, but I couldn't hear what he was saying. He sent them inside the house. I thought they must be going in to make a phone call or something. I don't remember them coming out ...

Bill: And then he took off in the car?

Warwick: Yeah, he had a big Pontiac. But the front door was open so I just figured, hey, they'd gone out the front door and gone down to the tram or something – he'd given them some money or something like that. I did go in the house but the kids weren't there. He later took off with all his bags in the back of the car.

Bill: But how long after he'd spoken to the kids did he take off in the car?

Warwick: About 20 minutes ... I didn't see the kids coming out of the house or get into the car. I didn't go in the house. They could have gone out the front door. Actually – actually, that's what I thought, I thought they went out the front door.

We used to manufacture surfboards and they used to sell the surfboards in these great big plastic bags, right, so they were about 10 foot long and Hank used to get these great big bags and put his dresses in them and they're made of really heavy duty PVC – really thick, almost like canvas bags.

Bill: Where would he be taking his dresses to?

Warwick: Oh, he had – he had a whole house full of them. He bought two houses up the road from [the factory].

Bill: So, he'd take them to these other houses?

Warwick: They were two old houses [on the street]. They were both used for manufacturing surfboards, but we didn't make any money out of making surfboards, so Hank sold the business and he kept one of the houses for doing all his sewing – he put his sewing machines in there. He'd import rolls and rolls of satin from Hong

Kong and he'd have it on a big stick ... he'd be pulling out these great big sheets of bloody satin.

There's a dump straight out the back [of that house] ... we used to dump all our [factory waste] there. We had a drop of about 12 feet from the front to the back. So, we just filled it all up with sand ... it was a 'shit pit'.

Bill: Did you think at any stage, whether it be a day, a month, six months, a year, at any stage later, that perhaps you should have maybe spoken to the police about what you'd seen that day?

Warwick: You know, I thought about it, but they made such a farce of the psychic and all the rest of it ... they were going to rip the floor out of the supermarket because this sheila said this is where the bodies are buried and all the rest of it, and nothing like that had ever happened in Glenelg before ... I thought, nah, I'm not going to be shown up as a dill just by saying anything, you know?

Bill: How long had you seen them for? How long were they standing and talking to Hank?

Warwick: Oh, only long enough until he took them inside. After that I came out of the cubby-house and went inside to see what was going on and the front door was open so I just assumed they left out the front door.

Bill: And then you didn't see them again after they went inside the house?

Warwick: No.

Bill: Did you become aware of the kids going missing the next day when all the –

Warwick: In the following week there was enormous publicity.

Bill: But you didn't tie it to the kids that you saw [in your backyard] for some time, you said?

Warwick: Not for 12 months, I'd say.

Bill: Do you think that he would have had it in him, you know him … have it in him to kill three innocent children like that?

Warwick: He wouldn't even think about it.

Bill: Tell me about the factory. It had a large dump behind the house there?

Warwick: You know, he had a four-acre dump – four acres of sand. And there was a bulldozer there, every day, just bulldozing it over. About 300, 400 metres away, there was about a 12 foot fall. All they did was dump there and then get the bulldozer out just to push it over the edge … every day, until eventually all that became the same level as the back fence.

Bill: And you thought the time of the day when you saw Hank loading the car was after 1 o'clock, or thereabouts I think you said.

Warwick: Yeah, I reckon it would be about that, 1 o'clock.

Bill: Okay. And, what, it was an hour or so later when he left?

Warwick: Something like that.

Bill: Were you there when he came back?

Warwick: No …

Bill: Is there anything that we haven't covered about this that you would like to cover?

Warwick: No, that's full … That's as much … About as much as I can remember, yeah.

Bill: A bit taxing on you, I understand, no. But you're willing to undergo hypnosis if you wish and …

Warwick: Yeah, if you wish.

Bill: Have any threats, promises or inducements been made by any person to you to do this and give this statement?

Warwick: No, they have not.

Bill: It's all true and accurate to the best of your knowledge and belief?

Warwick: It is, correct.

Bill: If you're required to give this evidence before some sort of court or tribunal would you be willing to tell them the same things you told me?

Warwick: Yes, I would.

Bill: Would you be willing to undergo hypnosis if you were required to in relation to this to see if there is something there?

Warwick: Yes.

* * *

A 'policeman's nose' they called it – old-fashioned intuition – the subconscious picking up of verbal and nonverbal clues that are inconsistent with someone telling the truth. For Bill, there was nothing in what Warwick had said that indicated he was making it all up.

'My feeling was, he was reliving what had happened,' Bill said. 'What really impressed me was that, on a number of occasions, he said it wasn't fair for him to be telling me this, because Hank wasn't here to defend himself. There was a sense of loyalty ... if he was out to destroy his father why did he say that? It was very compelling to me ... he hated his father, but he really loved him. He was defending his alleged attacker.'

Grappling with often-conflicting details didn't mean Warwick was lying, Bill explained. 'It means quite the opposite actually ... if this was a contrived story, he'd have it down pat and he would stick to it. Warwick was struggling to remember. And if he lied to Stuart 12 months ago, he'd have difficulty remembering those lies again to me – especially with so much alcohol and [prescription] drugs in his system.'

If it all hinged on Warwick, Bill pointed out, the story might not stand up in court, because he might crack under the pressure. 'There is an old saying in police circles,' Bill told me, 'that you can't pick your witnesses. But we still have this information and can act upon it.'

Warwick was tired after the interview. 'I didn't want to overdo it and put him under a lot stress,' Bill said. But he desperately wanted to do a video interview with Warwick, so that others could see what he was seeing. Warwick agreed to Bill videoing their next meeting and they agreed to catch up soon.

A couple of days later, Bill was back in Adelaide when he got a phone call from Warwick. His dreams and nightmares had started again.

'Amanda told me he'd had some very bad times reliving his abuse,' Bill recalled. 'The first thing Warwick said to me on the phone that day was, "Do you think I was involved in this?" It was a very strange thing to ask. Once again, if everything he said had been lies, I don't think he would have said that. He told the truth and desperately wanted us to believe he wasn't involved in some way. Someone who was lying wouldn't have cared. "No, we never thought that at all," I told him.'

Warwick rambled on for a while and said he didn't want to be involved in it anymore. Bill told him he was involved, explaining, 'We just have to get through this and see where it takes us …'

'I don't want to be involved,' Warwick replied.

'You are …'

Rather than handing over the recording of his interview with Warwick to the police, Bill decided to take another route. He gave the original dossier and a transcript of the interview to a South Australian-based member of Federal Parliament, and asked him to read all the information and see what he thought.

'This is amazing, Billy,' the Federal Member told him.

'He'd never seen any information like this before,' Bill said.

The Federal Member went to see SA Premier Mike Rann, and one of his media liaisons contacted SAPOL to say that someone needed to look into it. An Acting Superintendent came to Bill's office. The SAPOL officer told Bill they had already looked into Stuart's information and there was nothing to it.

'It took us months to get Warwick to talk to us,' Bill told the senior SAPOL officer, sitting in his office that day. It is well-documented that abused males distrust authority and do not want to speak to the police, Bill explained. Warwick would only open up about what he knew in a face-to-face interview, in a non-threatening environment, and Bill would be happy to be involved in setting up the meeting.

'Whatever you do,' Bill told the detective, in his typically straightforward manner, 'Don't just ring Warwick on the phone and go in "boots and all" about his father, the sexual abuse and what he alleges about the Beaumonts ... nothing will be gained from it.' He was told the police would handle it.

Chapter 19

A Public Inquiry

A SAPOL detective called Warwick Harrison in September 2009, more than three years after his ex-wife Amanda had first contacted us about his allegations, and two years after Stuart Mullins first sent his dossier to police. It had taken Stuart and Bill Hayes, with Amanda's assistance, a long time to develop a trusting relationship with Warwick to the point where the he felt safe enough to tell them about his abuse and what he knew about his father.

In passing this information on to SAPOL, Stuart and Bill stressed the importance of 'going in gently' with a 'kid gloves approach', because of Warwick's fragile physical and mental state. Once he had opened up and told others of his abuse, Warwick's nightmares returned and he started drinking again. His health quickly deteriorated, but he stabilised again when his public trustees bought him an apartment, and he was receiving support from Amanda.

Although Stuart and Bill both offered to be with Warwick when he was interviewed, the SAPOL detective instead contacted Queensland Police, who couldn't locate Warwick's new address. A Queensland sergeant rang Warwick and asked him to state his address. Warwick didn't know who this person was, and immediately worried it was someone from the newspapers. He refused to give out his address. He was then advised that police wished to speak with him about his information. He told police that he had said all he wanted to say to the private investigator and would not speak to police. Warwick, in a panic, called Amanda, and his childhood friend Steve Parker in Adelaide.

After he refused to speak to Queensland Police, a senior detective from SAPOL phoned Warwick from Adelaide. Again, Warwick insisted he had already told everything he knew about the Beaumont children to Bill Hayes. When pressed, Warwick told the senior police officer that when he saw his father 'dressing up' in satin, his father disowned him, and this is why he hated his father. The SAPOL detective formed the opinion that Warwick had made the rest of it up, although Stuart reminded him that Warwick had regularly visited sexual abuse clinics for therapy in the 1990s and early 2000s.

SAPOL told Stuart they had made extensive inquiries into the allegations being made. Stuart asked for more details about what inquiries had taken place. SAPOL told him they had called an ex in-law, who had been left a substantial amount of money in Hank's will (and had not wanted to talk to Stuart under any circumstances). The detective spoke to one of the people who was given a £1 note by Hank, to Hank's second wife Norma, and to some business associates. They did not speak to any of the other people in Stuart's dossier – not Warwick's son, friends, his second wife or any of his counsellors. They had not conducted a search of Hank's family home or his former business.

Stuart reminded the detective that he had spoken to many people regarding Hank and Warwick. Some had stated that Warwick was erratic, 'a spoilt rich kid' who hated his father with a passion from an early age. Others, however, said he was 'reliable, honest and when the pressure was on, trustworthy.' Stuart was sure Warwick was telling the truth about what he knew.

'It's hard to tell with people with mental illness,' the detective replied. 'Sometimes they genuinely believe what they are saying is true.'

But Warwick didn't have a mental illness, Stuart reminded him.

Soon after he'd been contacted by SAPOL, Warwick sold his apartment and, following a period of drinking heavily and living in motels, moved into a men's assisted care facility for invalid pensioners. His relationship with his former wife, Amanda, took a turn for the worse, and Warwick barred her from visiting him at his new address. Stuart suffered a similar rebuff when he tried to reconnect with Warwick via email and made the mistake of pressing him to tell his story to the police. Bill Hayes was still keen to get Warwick's allegations on video so he could show it to SAPOL, but when Bill rang him, Warwick became irate and said he didn't want to speak about it any more.

Knowing that in his present state, Warwick would not agree to another interview, Bill rang Amanda and said he would fly to Queensland, to work on a 'Plan B' to help Warwick tell his story. Amanda and Bill went to a local motel, where Warwick was staying before going into assisted care, and set up a time to film an interview with him. Amanda brought Warwick downstairs, but as soon as Bill saw him, he knew Warwick had been on a massive bender; he was dirty, dishevelled and smelling of alcohol. 'We spoke for a while and I was trying to motivate him to sort his life out,' Bill said. 'I felt truly sorry for him. It was so sad to see a man who had so much potential and ability in life, and to see what he became.'

Warwick would not agree to an interview. When it was time for Bill to leave, Warwick asked Bill if he was going to 'put these bastards in jail'. It was an interesting choice of word, 'bastards', Bill recalled later – was there more than one person involved?

'No, Warwick,' Bill said calmly. 'There's no one left to put in jail ... This is about finding the bodies of the children and returning them to their parents for a decent Christian burial.'

Warwick answered Bill straight away:'They're in the sandpit, Bill.'

It chilled Hayes to the bone; it was the same answer Warwick had given Bill six months before.'He firmly believes it to be true,' Bill told us. It was the same comment he'd made to Stuart 11 months before that, and to his own son over many years.

'That was a turning point for me,' Bill went on. 'If he had been lying about everything, why did he say that? It would have been easier for him to tell us nothing and send us on our way.'

* * *

Stuart also had a'Plan B.'He contacted Steve Van Aperen, a renowned forensic polygraph analyst, whose services have been widely used by police all over the world. Known as the 'human lie detector', with a BA (Criminal Justice Administration), Graduate Diploma (Security Management) and Forensic Polygraph Examiner MAPA, Steve was the first Victorian police officer to graduate from Western Oregon University in the USA as a certified polygraph examiner. Author of the book *The Truth About Lies*, he also trained with, and examined the polygraph testing and behavioural interview techniques of, the Los Angeles Police Department (LAPD) Polygraph Unit, the Los Angeles County Sheriff's Office and the Federal Bureau of Investigation (FBI).

Steve is now the director of Australian Polygraph Services. He has consulted for the Victoria Police Homicide Squad and the SAPOL Major Crime Squad. He has conducted a number of polygraph tests for homicide investigations, frauds, rapes, sexual assault and abuse cases, and advised on veracity issues among various other cases.

Stuart called Steve to discuss the case of the Beaumont children. He was impressed with the professionals we had spoken to, especially

Bill Hayes and some senior ex-SAPOL detectives, who had provided their opinion on what we'd uncovered. Steve and Stuart spoke at length over the phone before meeting in Melbourne. Steve agreed to listen to the 90-minute interview Bill Hayes had conducted with Warwick, keeping in mind the physical and psychological problems Warwick had been going through at the time.

After listening to the recording a number of times and taking copious notes, Steve had no hesitation in saying that, in his view, Warwick had been sexually abused over many years by his father. Warwick spoke clearly, in the first person, and was vivid in his memory of his father and the abuse he'd suffered, Steve said. Steve was unclear about Warwick's vagueness with regard to having seen the Beaumont children that day – but in the three years Stuart talked to Warwick, Warwick had never deviated from his story. Steve believed Warwick could be hiding something, or could have seen more than he was saying.

Steve Van Aperen remains in contact with Bill Hayes and Stuart about the case. There are question marks over the recording and several things need to be clarified. Steve would like to interview Warwick face to face, but he knows it would be difficult given Warwick's state of mind.

We spoke to a number of former Major Crime detectives over the years, who gave us advice on how to move forward with the information we had. We were encouraged to lobby SAPOL to apply for a general search warrant, especially in regard to the Harrison family home. In South Australia, a GSW doesn't have to be endorsed by the court; detectives and police officers may choose to use them under the following circumstances:

The police officer named in any such warrant may, at any time of the day or night, exercise all or any of the following powers:

(a) the officer may, with such assistants as he or she thinks necessary, enter into, break open and search any house, building, premises or place where he or she has reasonable cause to suspect that—

an offence has been recently committed, or is about to be committed; or there are stolen goods; or

there is anything that may afford evidence as to the commission of an offence; or

there is anything that may be intended to be used for the purpose of committing an offence …

The factory Hank owned and ran for decades is now abandoned, so a thorough search may be possible. 'It's a big place, so where do you start?' a former detective told us. 'You need to find where the sandpit was located in the 1960s, and then use the correct sonar equipment to check it out. If SAPOL declines to do it for any reason, because of a lack of funds and manpower for example, maybe the State Government would come to the party and finance it.'

This ex-detective was very helpful and we suspect he may even have passed our cause on to the Major Crime unit at SAPOL – because suddenly, in 2012, we were in communication with SAPOL again, this time from the top.

In 2012, Stuart Mullins was contacted by Grant Moyle, Head of Major Crime for SAPOL. Stuart suggested Moyle meet with investigator Bill Hayes, who could give him an overview of what they had discovered about Hank Harrison and Warwick's allegations. Even Moyle's attention was pricked when Stuart mentioned Thomas Hendrick's claim that Hank associated with known paedophiles, and the fact that Hank's family said 'he couldn't help himself' when he dressed in satin.

Moyle came highly recommended by the former detectives Stuart had spoken to over the years – he was not only well-liked, but well respected. Moyle said he had the file Stuart had sent in and that 'extensive enquiries' were being made into Warwick's allegations against his father.

Grant also discussed with Stuart the possibilities for carrying out ground scans at the factory site. The area had been covered in reinforced concrete and covered a wide area. SAPOL had finite resources, Moyle said, and where would they even start digging? Moyle noted SAPOL had a long backlog of crimes, including murders and abductions.

'SAPOL gets leads about the Beaumont case all the time,' Stuart said. 'It discredits everyone to have to go through this charade every year ... rouge theories, "visions" and revelations. They all get lumped in together.'

But Stuart also told Moyle that, after sitting on this information for seven years, we needed to act. We would publish what had been revealed to us by Warwick Harrison and what we had been able to discover.

By publishing Warwick's account, we hope that a public inquiry – a coronial inquest, for example – might be established to test the information provided to SAPOL, and that the State Government would be encouraged to fund an excavation of the factory site. We also need a credible and unbiased investigation of Warwick's claims. Having documented the fiasco of the Paringa Park warehouse excavation, which stretched out over forty years, we are not interested in fundraising or Citizen's Action groups. We want this investigation to proceed in the hands of SAPOL, who will follow proper police procedure.

As Steve Van Aperen recently remarked to us, 'With a book being published or a public inquiry, you only need one person to step forward and the house of cards comes crashing down ... this is how most cases are solved worldwide.'

One of the idiosyncrasies of the Beaumont case is that there has never been a public inquest into the events of 26 January 1966 because, according to SAPOL, the parents never requested one. A coronial inquest would be difficult for Grant and Nancy Beaumont, but it could also potentially solve the case and bring closure for them.

'There is never, ever one victim,' Amanda said, when I called to tell her we would be publishing this book. 'Hank wouldn't have stopped when he had abused Warwick … others would have suffered. I know Warwick cares for other people and he surprised me when he said, "All I have left of Dad is his name." Hank might even have involved Warwick in some way … I think he knows more than what he's saying … it's a defence mechanism.'

Amanda is philosophical about the prospect of all these allegations finally being revealed. 'During this whole saga, it's another pebble thrown in the pond and we're watching the ripples make their way to the shore.'

If there is an inquiry, others may come forward with pieces of the puzzle. Call it the Jimmy Savile effect. When the first allegations against Savile, a British TV personality, were raised in 2011, it opened a torrent of complaints and led to a public inquiry. Perhaps, if there was an inquiry into Warwick's allegations, other people would come forward about Hank, too.

Just before this book went to press, Stuart Mullins met a man at a barbecue, in his fifties, who had lived in Somerton during the mid 1960s. When he discovered Stuart was researching the Beaumont children, the man said he used to play with Jane Beaumont before she disappeared. She was a lovely girl, he said; he remembered the tricycle she rode.

The man later revealed to Stuart that a stranger had molested him on Henley Beach in 1965. He told Stuart that, when he was a small boy, a stranger rubbed himself against him in the surf one day.

When the stranger told the boy to swim under his legs, he closed his legs and held the boy under the water. He hated this and still remembered it clearly. Because he was upset, the man gave him some money (coins, not a £1 note) to buy a doughnut. The boy was enticed into the stranger's distinctive car and molested.

'I was lucky to get out alive,' the man confided in Stuart. He was still too traumatised to go into more detail. When he was asked if he remembered what type of car the stranger drove, the man told Stuart it was a khaki green, late 50s Holden ute, with a canopy – eerily similar to the car Hank's factory had owned, which he later gave to Warwick.

'Another coincidence?' Stuart asks. 'There's far too many in this story.'

A successful paedophile is an undetected one. In 1998, SAPOL published a profile of a child molester or abductor, compiled by its criminal profiler, Sergeant Robyn Filmer of the Violent Crime Unit. The profile was established in response to the seven unsolved child abductions in Adelaide, stretching back to the Beaumont children in 1966. Filmer stated that while it was impossible to 'categorise human behaviour into specific classifications that will be applicable to all situations,' it was possible to analyse the behaviour of offenders and identify the *type* of person who committed these crimes. The 'average' child molester is over 25 years of age, Filmer stated, and is male, single and lives alone or with parents. The offender is highly skilled in identifying children who are 'vulnerable' for attack.

According to a study of non-family child abductors who murder their victims by K. R. Beyer and J. O. Beasley (2003), a psychological profile of someone like Hank Harrison, would describe him as a 'situational' child molester who was 'morally indiscriminate' in his sexual preferences. This type of molester is an abuser of 'all available persons', children included, but they are not the overall goal. This type of person 'experiments sexually' (such as by dressing in satin) and is willing to try or do anything, such as bondage or transvestitism, but can also involve biological children or children by marriage because of their convenience.

An article by Jerome Elam, published in the *Washington Times* in 2011, states that 'one in eight males is a victim of abuse and a child has to tell seven adults about the abuse before he or she is taken seriously'. The male ego is conditioned by society not to show weakness, so the crime of molestation starts a life-long haemorrhaging of self-esteem that can be fatal if not treated. Rates of suicide among male victims of childhood sexual abuse are 14 times higher than the norm, and they are 38 times more likely to die from a drug overdose ... victims face a lifetime battle with depression, anger, addiction and possibly suicide ...'

In *Searching for the Beaumont Children*, I wrote, 'Time is working against solving the Beaumont Case. Many of the original witnesses – the 74-year-old woman who saw the children frolicking with the suspect, the elderly couple with their granddaughter, who spoke to the man – have passed away. There's a possibility that even the person responsible, described as being in his late 30s or early 40s in 1966, is also dead. Maybe all these years we have been searching for a phantom: someone who no longer exists.'

Almost 50 years on, the only suspect we have is the man seen playing with the Beaumont children on the morning they disappeared. On the available evidence, we believe Hank Harrison could be that man.

We call upon the South Australian State Government and SAPOL to conduct an inquiry or coronial inquest into these new allegations. By testing the evidence we have found, they may be able to determine, once and for all, who was responsible for the

Beaumont children's disappearance. We also believe that the evidence is strong enough to conduct a thorough search of Warwick Harrison's former family home in Glenelg, and the factory his father Hank once owned. We hope this book will encourage others to come forward with pieces of the jigsaw.

Perhaps then the mystery of the Beaumont children's disappearance will finally be solved.

Epilogue:

What Happened Next

With the publication of *The Satin Man* in 2013, for the first time in 30 years a new person of interest in the disappearance of the three Beaumont Children from Glenelg Beach in January 1966 had been identified. While it was our intention as authors to 'go public' in order for other people to come forward and, perhaps, provide new information which would prompt South Australian Police to conduct a coronial inquest, we were unprepared for the response to the book.

One of the first things that happened after the publication of the book was that the South Australian media soon worked out the real identity of the 'Satin Man'. Channel's 9's Brady Halls championed the story on *A Current Affair*, but Channel 7's Frank Pangello went one step further on *Today Tonight* and named the 'Satin Man'. The real 'Hank Harrison', a prominent South Australian, was revealed and his factory identified, which prompted a number of people only peripherally associated with the family in Glenelg to allege the book was 'lies' and the story was a complete fabrication. This was understandable, but what was equally amazing was the number of people who knew and worked with Hank and supported our story.

There was a concerted effort, however, by several people to attack the book in online forums. Some of them even dismissed Bill Hayes' credentials as a former member of Major Crime and misrepresented our own motivations in telling our story. One person questioned Stuart Mullins' credentials as a former teacher, and alleged that Nepean College of Advanced Education, in Kingswood NSW, 'never existed'. We both shook our heads at that one. Nepean CAE did exist the in 1970s and 1980s – I know because I graduated from there too – and it later became a campus of the University of Western Sydney.

But outside of this, some did come forward with other important pieces of the puzzle. Several people who knew the Harrison family confirmed that as far back as the early 1980s 'Warwick', Hank's son, had expressed his concerns that his father was involved in the disappearance of the three Beaumont children. Another family friend also knew of Hank's satin fetish. 'You have no idea what I have got myself into,' Norma, Hank's second wife, allegedly told him in the 1990s. When the man contacted us, he said our book pretty much reflected what he remembered about the Harrison family … dysfunctional, argumentative and secretive. Another friend of Warwick's, who confirmed that Hank's son hated his father with a passion, told us that he met Warwick's father years later when he worked as a barman in a 'gentleman's club' in Adelaide. He particularly remembered this night in the 1970s because all the men at the club, including Hank Harrison and several prominent people, were dressed in women's clothing.

After the book's publication, a removalist told us that he had transported 'items' from Harrison's Glenelg house after Hank was put into elderly care in the 1990s, including bundles of satin pyjamas. The removalist had offered to 'get rid of' the satin items, much to the relief of Hank's second wife, Norma, and took them to his home. He sent us as photo of one, which is reproduced in this book.

A painter-decorator who knew the Harrison family saw the

program on *A Current Affair* and although the 'Satin Man' was not yet identified, he knew who it was straight away. Sometime after Hank's death in the mid-2000s, the local man was asked by Hank's second wife to clean out the attic. Everything had to go, the man was told. A wooden walkway ran the length of the attic and appeared to be purposely built. There were shelves of books, old newspapers and various items of women's clothing as well as rolls and rolls of satin in the attic, the man later recalled.

The handyman said that at the back of the attic there was a room painted black which made it difficult to see from the manhole. The room was about three metres square in size and was made of sheet metal. The room had a sliding bolt on the door but the man didn't recall seeing a lock on it. The room was reachable via the wooden walkway which ran from the large manhole cover to the back corner of the attic. Inside the secreted room was a small fireplace and a stool.

Stuart asked the man if he could hear street traffic from the small room in the attic. His answer was no... the attic was very well insulated. Stuart asked if he made a loud noise in the room could it be heard from outside? Again, in his opinion, he said no. What was the secret room in the attic built for?

But the most important piece of new information was volunteered by two brothers, now in their 60s. The pair, one an engineer and the other a retired public servant, contacted us and said that in the summer of 1966, when they were still teenagers, they were asked by a man at a local factory to dig a large hole in the sand near the back gate. It was the same factory that Channel 7 had identified as being possibly involved in the disappearance of the children.

They were two local boys who lived close to the factory and often did odd jobs around the area. One of the brothers was saving to buy a car, because he was starting University which, he remembered, was in the first week of February 1966. They placed the time of this dig as being on the Australia Day holiday weekend, three days after the Beaumont children went missing.

The hole had to be dug with some urgency, they remembered, in the back corner of the factory near a large gate. It had to be finished by the end of the weekend but they were promised they would be 'very well paid'. The hole had to be approximately 6 feet deep (slightly less than two metres), a metre wide and about two metres long. It took the best part of two days to dig it, the pair later recalled, because the sides of the sandy soil kept falling in on them.

The unusual aspect of the job, the brother's remembered, was that they only had to dig the hole, not bury anything or fill it back in.

The factory was closed, with no one around to interrupt them and it was 'very, very hot.' The boys used shovels that were supplied by the factory. Several times during the day a car drove into the area and the driver just sat and stared at them while they worked. The man briefly spoke to the older brother ... the boys assumed he was the owner of the factory because he looked at the hole and he said he wanted it deeper. He then drove off.

The owner was a tall man, with brown wavy hair, they said, which matched the description of Hank Harrison. The brothers remember the man drove a large green car, with 'rear fins and lots of chrome'. The car Harrison drove at that time was an American import with large back fins and a lot of chrome.

There was a large gate at the back of the factory where the boys let themselves in and out over the weekend. After two days, the hole was completed and they simply left. Over the years, the brothers would often joke about 'the weird job' they'd done in the 1960s when they 'had to dig the grave for that factory guy'. There was no context to why they had to do that particular job, but after seeing the story on Channel 7 about the possible burial place for the Beaumont Children and then reading *The Satin Man*, it all appeared to fit together.

Private investigator Bill Hayes met with the two brothers separately and found them to be 'credible, intelligent, reliable and honest.' Both highly successful in their own fields, their stories matched. As retired detective Mostyn Matters later remarked, 'This is what a detective wishes for in "cold cases" such as this … corroborating evidence. It was certainly no coincidence.'

The obvious question was why didn't the brothers go to SAPOL with their information? One of the brothers had contracted the 'Crime Stoppers' phone line after seeing the Channel 7 report about the factory on Today Tonight and telling a friend, who was a serving police officer, what they had experienced back in 1966. The reason he contacted the authors was that in the weeks since, he had not heard back from Crime Stoppers. By sheer coincidence, on the day the brothers met with Bill Hayes in Adelaide they were contacted by SAPOL. In their defence, SAPOL receive a large amount of information to sift through and to prioritise so delays are inevitable.

It would be seven weeks, however, before SAPOL would act on the brothers' information and conduct a dig at the factory. The area was not secured or cordoned off.

The brothers met with a detective working on the 'Beaumont' cold case at the factory individually on different days. More than four decades had passed and the brothers needed to get their bearings. The detective was 'a nice enough bloke', one of the brothers later remarked, but he gave the impression that his mind was already made up on this matter. They were wasting their time.

The brothers believed they had dug the hole in the northeast corner of the factory inside the back gates. One of them met the detective and the plant manager at the front office and was actually taken to another part of the factory. It didn't seem like the same area, he remarked, and when he was told by the site manager that the ground they were standing on was only purchased from the adjoining property 15 years previously, he thought they were being taken for fools.

One of the brothers asked again to be taken to the northeast corner of the factory and was then asked to 'pinpoint' to within a metre where they thought the hole was originally dug back in 1966. One brother was unsure and could only identify a general area. The other brother, independently of his sibling, stood on a spot that he believed was within a metre of where they had originally dug the hole. After describing the dimensions of the hole they had dug to the detective, he was shown off the property.

The area had changed a lot since 1966. For one, the soil colour was different from what the brothers remembered. A manager of the factory later told the brothers the area where they had dug the original hole had been back-filled with about a metre of sand and soil in the late 60s, early 70s at the direction of Hank Harrison for no apparent reason. The back-filling caused so many problems with the spill falling onto the internal roadway that the factory had to build a retaining wall.

In October 2014, SAPOL used ground sonar to identify a small area that may have been 'the hole' as it appeared to show the 'straight sides' of a hole that had previously been dug. The only problem was, the soil was very sandy and the brothers had a lot of trouble digging the hole because the walls kept crumbling in … hardly the straight sides of a neatly excavated grave. Could this have been the same hole? And how deep were they were going to dig … three metres? Not likely.

The most frustrating thing about the subsequent police dig was that the brothers weren't on site when the police excavated the site so they could identify the original hole. Following their excavation, SAPOL were quick to conduct a press conference and declare that nothing had been found. No wonder, because they weren't looking in the right place, or digging deep enough. By missing the hole by just a metre, they might as well have missed it by a mile. Many believe SAPOL should have dug up the entire back site.

The questions remain. Why would a factory owner of wealth and prominence ask two brothers to dig a hole 6ft long, 3ft wide and 6ft deep – roughly two cubic metres – at the back of the factory three days after the Beaumont children went missing? And why on the weekend when no one was around? Hank Harrison had a factory full of staff that could have done this for him. What was he putting in the hole? And why was he so secretive about it? One thing we have learned about Hank Harrison is that he had to have complete control and command of a situation. What better place to hide three bodies than where he could watch over them every single day.

Watching all of this unfold was a man who had remained relatively quiet during the previous twelve months. Warwick, now clean and sober, contacted his old friend Steve Parker in Adelaide. 'They dug in the wrong spot,' were his first words. Warwick was back in the land of the living, ready perhaps to reconcile at last with his troubled past. As someone later commented to us, 'No man who was making this up would dare be so tormented and worried and wanting the facts to be corrected.'

And this is the paradox of the entire case. Having gone public with is story, and exposing his family history and his allegations to so much scrutiny, observation and even public ridicule, one could have been forgiven for thinking that Warwick would have been angry, embarrassed even, now that his darkest secrets – or lies – had been laid bare. But Warwick wasn't angry. He was relieved. He had told the truth, and now it was up to the police to investigate. He had gone as far as his courage, his convictions and his demons, would let him. He was free of it.

Warwick also made contact with Stuart again after an absence of

18 months. He even started talking to his ex-wife Amanda. He had a new apartment, was being looked after by conservators and was getting the medical support he needed. He was friendly, and open to new possibilities in life ... not someone who was hiding from the world because he had constructed an enormous lie.

Stuart and Warwick started to discuss the case again – 'you don't know the half of it,' Warwick told him, 'and the hell I've been through' – and he planned to formally interview Warwick again, but that was some time off into the future. He was, instead, enjoying Warwick's company ... his self-deprecating humour, his intelligence. Warwick was no angel, he was the first to admit that, but he never backed down on his assertion that his father was involved in the disappearance of the Beaumont children.

Perhaps there was a future for Warwick after all.

Late last year, Stuart invited Warwick to lunch. Moss Matters was in Queensland on holiday and Stuart wanted the pair to finally meet. Warwick's old friend Steve was there too. Warwick was in good health at the time and jumped at the chance to go out and enjoy lunch with friendly company. Warwick was in fine form, Stuart later observed, and got on famously with retired detective Matters. When Warwick learned that Matters was on duty at Glenelg the day the three Beaumont Children disappeared, he asked lots of questions and was genuinely impressed with what Matters knew about the case – this was not someone who was shying away from an elaborate lie or who had anything to hide. Warwick wanted to talk about the case.

After Warwick left the lunch, Matters remarked to Stuart that he was convinced Warwick was telling the truth about what happened that day when the Beaumont children went missing. Call it a policeman's instinct. Matters could smell a fake from a mile away, just as Bill Hayes could, and Warwick was no fake. All that was needed was for SAPOL to interview Warwick officially and they could take it from there.

Then, in the middle of 2015, Warwick passed away suddenly. It appeared he had fallen and bumped his head. There was a lot of blood on the floor and it was several days before anyone noticed that he was not answering his calls. Warwick was on a myriad of prescription medication, including anti-depressants, but whatever the reason the son of the Satin Man was dead. Although there was always the hope that Warwick would regain his health and shine further light on his allegations, that hope was now dashed. At least Warwick is in a much happier place.

SAPOL believe the matter concerning the 'Satin Man' is now closed. But how can that be the case when the people close to the Harrison family have still not been interviewed? Warwick's ex-wife, his son and close friends have still never been interviewed by SAPOL, nor has Billy Hayes, Stuart or myself.

Just as SAPOL believed the matter concerning the 'Satin Man' was closed, Channel 7 took up the story over the summer of 2017–2018. Using state of the art sonar technology, a documentary team was given permission by the owners of the factory at North Plympton to investigate irregularities in the topography that might indicate a burial site.

Using the information supplied by the two teenagers who dug a trench on the site back in 1966, Channel 7 identified an area on the eastern boundary of the factory that resembled a trench. With a commitment from the media station to partially finance the dig, SAPOL announced the planned excavation of the factory for February 2018.

A large news contingent watched the dig, with around-the-clock updates and live crosses across the nation. Reporters were clambering over each other to get an angle on the story, until the sobering realisation would dawn that the police were searching for the remains of three little children.

The only items found that day in the excavated area, however, were the bones of dead animals and rubbish – it was an old rubbish trench used by farmers to bury dead animals and burn off waste. Hopes had been dashed, but as I later remarked to one of the media people on site, 'just because the children weren't found doesn't mean they're not there.'

Warwick Harrison had always told us the children were buried in the sandpit, on the other side of the factory … not here on the boundary. Until that area had been excavated – indeed the whole two hectares of the factory – this story would never be over.

But at last SAPOL was taking the allegations in this book seriously. Shortly before the dig they publicly stated that a deceased Adelaide man – who we have declined to name for legal reasons but whose identity is widely known in the media – was now a 'person of interest' in their on-going investigation into the children's disappearance.

If Glenelg police had known back in 1966 that a local man who fitted the description of the Beaumont suspect and had allegedly abused his own son as part of an overwhelming satin fetish – a wealthy, well-connected man who was known to give out £1 notes to children – was living 250 metres from where the Beaumont children disappeared from Colley Reserve on Australia Day, wouldn't they have at least visited his home, searched the house and investigated his place of work?

Well, they know now.

Alan Whiticker, 2021

The Beaumont Children Case

A Timeline of Events

1966

26 January
Jane, Arnna and Grant Beaumont travel
to Glenelg Beach, southwest of Adelaide,
at 10.00am. They are reported missing
by their parents that evening.

27 January
Police begin searching Glenelg/
Brighton beaches and around the
surrounding esplanade. ADS7 set up
a mobile broadcast studio to transmit
updates of the search.

28 January
The first descriptions of the children
are published – their clothing, ages and
final movements.

29 January
A £500 reward is posted by the SA
Government. First clue is provided
by a 74-year-old woman, who saw the
children playing under the sprinklers
with a tall, 30-year-old man.

31 January
Adelaide Advertiser artist Peter von
Czarnecki provides first sketch of the
main suspect.

2 February
Police conduct a house-to-house
search for the missing children.
An elderly couple tells police they had
a conversation with the man seen with
the Beaumonts at Glenelg.

3 February
Patawalonga boat haven is drained and
searched for the bodies of the missing
children.

4 February
Two men are prosecuted for false
reports regarding the whereabouts of
the missing children.

11 February
Retired Sydney detective Ray Kelly arrives in Adelaide to help the Beaumont investigation. He leaves after just one day.

16 February
The Suburban Taxi Service announce the foundation of a public fund to support the Beaumont family.

18 February
Hobart police launch a search for a man in the Sandy Bay area who fits the description of the 'Beaumont' suspect.

23 February
Twelve police cadets search Marion Council dump, after a man says he has found a 'shallow grave'. Nothing is found during a three-day search.

12 March
Life-sized models of the three missing children, in the clothes they wore to Glenelg Beach, are exhibited at the Sydney Easter Show.

14 March
For the first time, police acknowledge the theory that the children could have known their abductor.

15 July
The total reward for information regarding the missing children is raised

to $10,000 after Adelaide businessman Barry Blackwell donates $2,000.

1 August
Dutch clairvoyant Gerard Croiset is consulted for the first time; he says the children are 'buried in a cave'. He asks for film and photographs of Glenelg to be sent to him in the Netherlands.

7 August
Croiset states the children 'lie buried in sand two kilometres [about 1¼ miles] from where they were seen near a merry-go-round at Glenelg Beach'.

9 August
Civilian volunteers resume searching the Glenelg and Brighton areas following the revelations by Gerard Croiset.

25 September
Dr D. B. Hendrickson contacts Croiset and informs the clairvoyant of diggings he has carried out on the grounds of the Minda Home at Brighton. Croiset tells Hendrickson that he is 'close'.

28 September
Kaniva policeman Senior Constable Bob Grose overhears a telephone conversation in which the Beaumont children are said to be returning from Hobart.

9 October
Jim Beaumont and Brian Taylor travel to Kaniva to investigate the phone call Grose overheard, after SA Police say that the reference to the Beaumonts was not a hoax.

10 October
Tonnes of rubble and sand are removed from the grounds of the Minda Home in Brighton when Gerard Croiset nominates this as the children's burial site.

12 October
Two South Australian come forward to clear up the Kaniva connection: they were talking about family friends.

8 November
Dutch clairvoyant Gerard Croiset arrives in Adelaide. He begins retracing the children's final steps through Glenelg the following day.

10 November
Croiset investigates the Minda Home for clues of the children's whereabouts, but fails to nominate any one spot.

11 November
Croiset announces that the remains of children are buried under the floor of a warehouse in the Adelaide suburb of Paringa Park. He flies out of the country that day.

15 November
SA Premier Frank Walsh announces his Government will not subsidise the excavation of the warehouse.

1967

26 January
On the first anniversary of the disappearance, a Citizen's Action Committee announces it will raise funds to excavate the Paringa Park warehouse.

1 March
Excavation begins on the floor of the Paringa Park warehouse.

8 March
'Rubbish' found in one of the cavities under the floor of the warehouse is ruled out of having anything to do with the missing children.

10 March
Excavation of the floor of the warehouse finishes, with no sign of the Beaumont children.

7 September
Adelaide detectives deny that they are investigating a former mental patient from Glenside Hospital in relation to the whereabouts of the missing children

1968

5 January
Surplus money raised to excavate
the Paringa Park warehouse by the
Citizens Action Committee is donated
to charity.

26 February
Detective Sergeant Stan Swaine goes
with Jim and Nancy Beaumont to
Dandenong, to meet 'a man' who is
going to return their children. Nobody
shows up, and it is later proven to be
an elaborate hoax.

18 March
Police abandon a search on Mud
Island in Port Phillip Bay, 80 km south
of Melbourne, after investigating an
anonymous letter.

3 April
Police search a scout camp at Anglesea,
near Geelong (Victoria) after a woman
reports a possible gravesite. It turns
out to be a mound of rubbish.

20 September
The crew of the Australian freighter
Devon are questioned in Auckland,
NZ. The ship was docked in
Adelaide when the Beaumont
children went missing, and later
in Melbourne when a young girl
disappeared.

1970

12 April
Melbourne police question convicted
murderer, 21-year-old Derek Percy,
about the Wanda Beach murders of
1965 and the disappearance of the
Beaumont children.

1971

30 January
SA police search vacant land at
O'Halloran Hill after a tip-off about
the Beaumont Children.

1972

10 May
Dr George Duncan, a gay university
lecturer, drowns after being bashed
and thrown into the Torrens by several
men. Another man is rescued by a
passer-by, 26-year-old accountant
Bevan von Einem.

1973

25 August
Eleven-year-old Joanne Ratcliffe and
four-year-old Kirste Gordon are
abducted from the Adelaide Oval
by an unknown man during a South
Australian AFL match.

28 August
First report links the disappearance
of two young girls from the Adelaide
Oval to the Beaumont case.

1 September

An artist's sketch of the man seen walking from the Adelaide Oval with the missing girls bears an uncanny resemblance to the suspect seen with the three Beaumont children at Glenelg Beach in 1966.

1974

6 July

Gerard Croiset Junior, the son of the Dutch clairvoyant who came to Adelaide in 1966, predicts that the man who abducted the two girls from the Adelaide Oval will strike again 'within 16 days'. He is wrong.

1978

28 January

Following the 12th anniversary of the Beaumont children's disappearance, real estate millionaire Con Polites advocates the further excavation of the Paringa Park warehouse.

26 July

After speaking to British spiritualist Doris Stokes, Les Ratcliffe believes he knows the name of the man who took his daughter and where her remains are buried.

31 July

Gerard Croiset Junior visits Adelaide and vows to solve the five-year-old

Ratcliffe–Gordon disappearance from the Adelaide Oval. He doesn't.

1979

10 July

A Coronial Inquest hears that Adelaide Oval officials refused to broadcast that the two girls were missing during the match in 1973.

1980

14 December

In an interview with journalist Dick Wordley, Les Ratcliffe reveals that he is dying of cancer and asks his daughter's abductor to contact him. He hears nothing.

1981

1 February

Les Ratcliffe, the father of one of the girls abducted from the Adelaide Oval in 1973, dies of cancer. Before his death, he pens an open letter to the people of Adelaide, asking them not to forget its missing children.

2 December

Police investigate reports by a woman claiming she played with the three Beaumont children on the day they disappeared and knows why they left the beach. No new evidence is uncovered.

7 December
SAPOL detectives allow forensic examination of 'the Dandenong letters', allegedly written by Jane Beaumont to her parents in 1968.

1983

6 January
Ten-year-old Louise Bell is abducted from her Hackem West home.
No trace of the child is found despite an extensive search.

24 July
The body of 15-year-old Richard Kelvin is found, seven weeks after he went missing from a public bus stop. Kelvin had been dead only two weeks and had obviously been kept alive by his abductor.

3 November
Bevan Spencer von Einem is arrested for the murder of Richard Kelvin and suspected of being involved in the deaths of four other young men.

1985

12 January
A woman claims that three children living in Kalgoorlie in the late 1960s were the Beaumonts. Police rule out the claim after they identify the people, now living in Geraldton, WA.

1986

12 March
Council workers find a dumped file of newspaper clippings, related to the Beaumont case. Police investigate when annotations on the clippings comment on where the children's bodies may be buried.

13 March
An Adelaide family comes forward and says that they dumped the annotated news clippings, which belonged to an elderly family member who was obsessed by the case.

1990

2 February
Major Crime Squad detectives and members of the Underwater Recovery Unit search the Myponga Reservoir, but refuse to confirm or deny whether they are looking for the remains of the Beaumont children.

23 February
Journalist Dick Wordley says the postman who spoke to Jim Beaumont in Dandenong in 1968 may hold the key to the fate of the children.

24 February
Former Homicide Detective Jack Zeunert states that a religious sect operated in the Adelaide Hills in the 1970s, and that it was not unreasonable to suggest that children

could have been kidnapped or handed over to it.

17 March
Suppression orders are lifted during the trial of Bevan von Einem. Allegations that he was responsible for as many as 10 murders, including the Beaumont and the Adelaide Oval victims, and that their bodies were dumped at Myponga Reservoir, are revealed.

27 March
Adelaide clairvoyant June Cox says she knows the burial place of the Beaumont children, as well that of Joanne Ratcliffe and Kirste Gordon. Although she tells police the 'children were calling her', nothing is found.

28 May
The News computer artist Bette Clarke digitally ages photos of the Beaumonts to determine what they would look like if they were still alive.

1992

6 June
A Melbourne man, who was 17 in 1968, admits that he sent the 'Dandenong' letters to Jim and Nancy Beaumont. Advances in fingerprint technology had identified him.

7 October
Rhianna Barreau, aged 12, is taken from her Morphett Vale home.

1995

16 December
Adelaide millionaire Con Polites advocates the use of sonar equipment to solve the mystery of the Paringa Park warehouse once and for all.

1996

26 January
Dame Idina Probyn uses the 30th anniversary of the children's disappearance to appeal for further excavation of the warehouse. She believes the children went there 'for a picnic' and were accidentally buried.

1 May
Workmen begin drilling the cement floor of the Paringa Park warehouse, searching for signs of the Beaumont children. The dig lasts almost five months but no new evidence is found.

26 May
Former SA Deputy Commissioner Geoffrey Leane, who died in 1990, revealed to his family that he believed the Beaumont children had been abducted and their remains discovered in an abandoned shipping container in an overseas port. SAPOL dismiss the claims.

1997

2 February
Human bones found behind a Glenelg service station in Brighton Road in

1990 are found to belong to a 40-year-old Aboriginal man. Further bones are recovered, but they do not belong to the Beaumont children.

6 August

Ex-detective Stan Swaine declares that the Beaumont children were handed over to a cult and that he has found 'Jane' living in Canberra. The woman is later awarded an AVO against the Adelaide investigator.

1998

5 December

86-year-old Queensland man Arthur Brown is charged with the murders of Judith and Susan Mackay in 1970, as well as a number of sexual assaults on members of his own family. Brown resembles the suspect in the Beaumont (1966) and the Adelaide Oval (1973) cases, but all charges are eventually dropped against him because of his age and ill health.

2004

12 May

Police in NZ investigate a man's claims that the Beaumont children were kidnapped and raised in Dunedin. The Australian media latches onto the story but it is proved to be untrue.

14 May

Victorian police confirm that they are reinvestigating the movements of murderer Derek Percy, who was jailed in 1970, in regard to several unsolved crimes including the Beaumont children. Percy, however, was only 17 in January 1966 and cannot be placed at Glenelg.

23 May

NZ Police rule out any suggestion that locals Judith Hewitt and Albert Larson are the missing Beaumont children. Both have NZ birth certificates.

2005

June

The reward for evidence leading to the conviction of the man responsible for the Beaumont abduction is increased from $10,000 to $100,000.

2006

26 January

The fortieth anniversary of the disappearance of the three Beaumont children from Glenelg Beach sees the publication of *Searching for the Beaumont Children*.

2006

6 October

The ABC broadcasts the long-delayed documentary *The Fisherman*, which suggests that convicted child killer James O'Neill was responsible for the Beaumont abductions.

2007

26 April
Foxtel's Crime & Investigation channel airs a documentary on the Beaumont children, featuring an Adelaide family's allegations that their father was involved in the murder of the Beaumont children. No charges are laid.

30 August
Derek Percy is questioned by Victorian police after new evidence, discovered among his possessions in a Melbourne storage unit, links him to several unsolved crimes involving children.

22 September
Police again question Bevan von Einem regarding the Beaumont Case and the Adelaide Oval abductions. It is revealed that an internal police report from 1989 identified von Einem as a suspect in the unsolved cases.

2 November
Bevan von Einem completes the non-parole part of his 36-year-sentence for the murder of Richard Kelvin but the SA Government declines to set a parole date.

2008

28 October:
The SA Government announces the doubling of the reward to solve the Beaumont children's disappearance, to $200,000.

2009

12 December
The inquest into the 1968 disappearance of St Kilda girl Linda Stilwell is adjourned when peripheral Beaumont suspect Derek Percy is not compelled to give evidence.

2011

2 October
A Channel 7 report links Derek Percy to the Beaumont Case in 1966, despite the fact that Percy was 17 years old at the time and his family deny ever going to Glenelg.

2012

25 January
David Estes of Irvine, Kentucky (USA) claims that he is Grant Beaumont. SAPOL are aware of Estes' claims. Unsurprisingly, he has failed to send supporting evidence.

2013

June
After new claims made by a Glenelg family, *The Satin Man* is published. The book investigates whether a local man may have been responsible for the Beaumont abductions, and buried the children, as alleged, in an Adelaide factory.

July
Channel 7 journalist Frank Pangello reveals to identity of the Satin Man

on *Today Tonight*. As a result, many people come forward with other pieces of information.

October
Two brothers who were teenagers in 1966 tell SAPOL that on the Australia Day holiday weekend in 1966 they were asked by the owner of a local factory to dig a hole 6ft deep, 3ft wide and 6ft long in the northeast corner of the site.

23 November
Acting on information from two members of the public, SAPOL excavates a small section of a local factory after using ground penetrating sonar technology. Nothing is found.

2015

March
Fresh information in the 1973 abduction of Joanne Ratcliffe and Kirste Gordon from Adelaide Oval implicate a North Adelaide family and a property at Yatina in the north of the state. Police excavate a disued bunker in the Adelaide suburb of Prospect but nothing related to the unsolved case is found.

April
Warwick Harrison, the son of the 'Satin Man', passes away suddenly at the age of 65. He was never formally interviewed by SAPOL.

2016

26 January
50th anniversary of the disappearance of the three Beaumont children from Glenelg Beach. SAPOL increases the reward for information regard this case to $1,000,000.

2018

24 January
Major Crime detectives name deceased Adelaide man Harry Phipps as 'a person of interest' in the disappearance of the three Beaumont children in 1966.

2 February
SAPOL and Channel 7 excavate an area of a North Plympton factory site, but only find animal bones and rubbish.

2019

16 September
Nancy Beaumont dies age 92 in an Glengowie nursing home with the mystery of her missing children still unsolved.

2021

26 January
Fifty-fifth anniversary of the disappearance of the three Beaumont Children from Glenelg Beach. The case remains an open investigation.